WITHDRAWN

von Riesen Library
McCook Community College

MARK THAYER

GETTING COLLEGE DONE:

MANAGE YOUR WORK, LIVE YOUR LIFE, AND GET THE MOST OUT OF YOUR COLLEGE EXPERIENCE

49° NORTH PRESS

Copyright © 2014 by Mark Thayer. All rights reserved.

PUBLISHED BY
49° North Press
Livermore, CA

ISBN 978-0-9908755-0-5

Contents

The Challenge Defined 9

Set Up Your Tools 15

The Workflow Management Process 21

Life Will Not Go as Planned 35

Procrastination, Work Ethic, and Winning the Internal Game 47

The Reality of the Student Job 57

For Advanced Practitioners 63

A Few Warnings, a Little Advice, and A Lot of Encouragement 73

Afterword 85

Bibliography 87

Preface

This is a book about *conscious choice*.

This is not a book about how to study, nor is it about getting your bachelor's degree in a year.

It's not a book about time management; time cannot be managed. It's not about hacking the latest calendar app on your smartphone.

This book is about how you take responsibility for deciding what you're going to do with the 168 hours you will be given this week. It's about actually *doing it*—living your life in accordance with your decisions, per your priorities, with full awareness of the benefits and consequences.

This book is about crafting the life you want in college. Along the way, you'll learn something about the kind of person you will need (and want) to be to be able to craft that life.

Your first choice is to accept the responsibility for your college life (and outcomes), or not. If you want to be the architect of your life, I think I can help you. If not, put this book down and go do something else.

The Challenge Defined

Think back and remember how many times you were up after midnight last semester, pushing yourself to finish an assignment or cram for an exam. How many times were you faced with the choice of getting the work done or participating in a non-academic activity that was important to you? Go further—think back on your overall academic experience thus far. Is your GPA as good as you think it could or should be? Do you think you are in control of your life, or are you being swept along by tides and currents with little ability to steer in the direction you wish to go?

Do you like your life now, or have you decided that you'll tough it out until graduation, and start your life then?

If your answers were largely positive—life is good, you're getting the results you want, stress is under control, and you can do all the things that matter to you—then give this book to someone else. Keep doing whatever it is that you're doing. Drop me a note and tell me how you do it, and don't fix what's not broken.

If your answers were completely negative, then we have a lot to discuss. Be of stout heart and good cheer. There are things you can do and skills you can learn that will make your life better.

Chances are you're somewhere in the middle. You had several late nights and the odd all-nighter as finals approached. There were times—not too many, but more than you would have liked—when you disappointed people because you had to forego an important non-academic activity in order to dig yourself out of a hole. The tough part is that the hole was largely of your own creation, because you put off important work time for what, in hindsight, were silly reasons. You probably have a nagging sense that your GPA could be better—not that it's bad now, but a few ticks higher might open a few more doors for you as you get close to graduation. Life could be more fully under your control. You could be getting a little more out of your college experience.

My guess is that you don't know where to start. You may have experimented with a calendar or planner application on your laptop or smartphone, but you could never quite make it work effectively in the context of everything going on in your life.

I don't want to belabor the obvious; you're familiar with the problem. You also likely know that you're not the only one facing this challenge. You have avoided it (so far), but maybe you've seen a few cases of real burnout. Then there's binge drinking, drug use, or worse.

The problem is pervasive—you can find examples on every college campus—and it is also persistent. The situation doesn't improve much as students make their way through the years toward graduation.

Do you like living this way?

We have touched briefly on the costs of a life not fully under control: late nights, too much stress, foregone activities, a GPA not as good as you think it should be. The degree of these costs can be extreme. Burnout is no small thing, and a full recovery is rare—not because of a lack of ability, but rather due to a shattered self-confidence that makes it easy to give in to the temptation of procrastination. There are longer-term costs. College is expensive, even at state schools. Scholarships and loans on favorable terms come with GPA strings attached. A lower-than-ideal GPA can cause major stress by itself, adding pressure to a situation where there is already enough. Further out, a mediocre GPA can hurt your chances to get into the grad school want. It can make it much harder for the new graduate—with loans to repay—to land a good entry level job.

None of this is news to anyone who is in college, who has children in college, or knows someone in college. The symptoms, problems, and consequences are all obvious. Can we identify causes? Will knowing this help us to create solutions? Is a solution possible?

I think we can identify causes well enough that we can proceed to the more important work, which is crafting and implementing solutions.

After years of working with my son and daughter and their friends, some patterns emerge. The first problem is that college is really nothing like high school, but students act as if it were. In high school, your schedule is not only fixed but filled; a high school schedule has little unstructured time. At the college level, a five course, fifteen credit hour schedule will mean 15–17 contact hours of class time per week. In high school, there was likely a teacher, counselor, or administrator around to "guide" you as to what to do with those few blocks of free time in your schedule. At the college level, no one cares what you do with unscheduled time.

The time horizon of assignments is different in college. Most high school assignments are completed before the next meeting of that class. As you progressed from your freshman to your senior year, the mix shifted, and there were more assignments of midterm (1–2 weeks) and long-term (1–2 months, or an entire term or semester), but it remained that most assigned work was fairly short-term (less than a week). In college, you will have reading assignments between classes that will never be formally "assigned" but you will be expected to complete them before the next class. Assignments with deliverables will range from a week (e.g., problem sets in hard sciences, mathematics, or engineering) to papers or small projects (2–4 weeks), to long projects (two months to an entire semester). Again, no one will be pushing you to pay attention to the longer-term work, which will make up a greater percentage of your workload than it did in high school.

You can see the immediate problem. The challenge of managing your life in high school is comparatively simple; decisions have been made for you. In college, more than half of the hours within the typical work week are "whitespace" time—uncommitted blocks of time that you have to decide how to use. Whatever methods you used to track assignments in high school will not scale well to the challenges of a college workload. Most high school students come to college lacking any real skills of work and life management.

The second major cause involves attitude and perception. Most high school students come to college or university with either unrealistic expectations or no idea as to the demands of a serious college workload—the realities of the college student "job." At the risk of oversimplifying, most high school students come to college expecting a larger, amplified, and more stimulating version of high school. There is a vague understanding that there will be work required, perhaps quite a good deal of it. The work will get squeezed, somehow, in between the time demands of all the other exciting things that await.

That's harsh, and finger-wagging is not my intent. Students contemplating a technical major or a pre-professional program know they are in for serious work. But they still bring high school ideas about the student "job" to the college environment. Combine this disconnect between perception and reality with minimal personal management skills and a campus full of temptation and diversion, and the least we can say is that the odds are not in the student's favor.

The thread that connects these two major challenges, and is the beginning of the path to a solution, is the idea of *conscious choice*. Failure to understand and respect the reality of the college job leaves the student unaware of the *need* to make hard choices about when, where, and how he will get the work done, what extra "stuff" of life is important and has to find its way onto the calendar (and what's *not* important), about relationships, about priorities. The first problem—the lack of personal management skills—leaves the student with no idea *how* to go about making these choices in a rational manner, consistent with priorities.

Given this powerful (dangerous?) combination, it is a credit to many students that they survive and achieve a degree of success. But it comes at a great cost, the greatest of which is a college experience not fully lived.

This book is my attempt to refute the seeming inevitability of the problem. Let's define success in college to mean optimizing your life based on your priorities—you decide what tradeoffs to make between academics, social life, and personal growth. Given this, I am convinced that your success has little to do with intelligence or other inherent characteristics. You need to learn a few simple skills. You need to work at cultivating some new attitudes and developing a few habits. If you're willing to put in the effort, you can be successful *on your terms*.

Assume we agree on the nature of the problem, and the costs and consequences that come with it. Assume further that we can specify a cure. The cure will have its own costs. It will require energy and attention throughout your academic career. The amount of energy and attention required will decline as the skills improve and habits are established. It might require changing some behaviors and a willingness to try new ones. You might, depending on the severity of your own case, have to confront some less-than-perfect aspects of your work habits. The cure might require the self-administration of a little "tough love."

Is it worth it? Consider:

- How would your life be better if, on most days, you were able to wrap up most of your academic work before dinner?

- How would your life be better if you could enjoy a nice dinner with friends on a regular basis, unworried that you're taking time away from your work?

- How would your life change if you enjoyed regular sleep and did not have to be up trying to finish work at 3:00AM?

- What might change for you if your GPA were as good as you think it could be?

- How much more real learning would you get out of your college experience if you could take the stress out of managing your workload?

- Finally—how would it feel to be living life according to your priorities and fully under your conscious control?

I can't (and won't) answer these for you, and I have no magic wand with which to make these things happen effortlessly. You will have to inject some energy. But I am convinced that these benefits are available to any student willing to implement the ideas we will discuss. The greatest benefit of all is knowing that you will have lived your college life on your terms, and will have made the most of the experience.

The cure has three parts:

- **mechanics**—how to get your arms around everything and make decisions as to how you're going to do it all (or not). This is straightforward stuff, but if you've never done it before, it will take a little practice.

- **work ethic**—we will confront the realities of the college student "job" and start cultivating habits and attitudes that are critical to your success. You will have to pay attention to nurturing these habits over the course of your academic career, but this is the powerful lever that can make big changes in the quality of your life.

- **"going pro"**—this is combining all the mechanics, habits, and attitudes such that you take full ownership and responsibility for your life as a student. It does not happen immediately. The "pro" concept serves as a powerful motivator while you are walking the path, and is directly applicable to life after college.

In my experience discussing and refining these ideas with students traditional and non-traditional, young and old(er), the best way to realize these benefits is to commit fully—to embrace the idea of taking full control of your life, right now. To get started:

- I will use direct language ("do it this way") for brevity and to get you started as quickly as possible.

- Please do what I ask you to do for an entire term or semester before making any changes. Make changes (and you should) after you have gained some experience.

- Be patient, especially with yourself. The hard part is not the mechanics but changing your behavior.

- *Make this a team sport.* The students I have known who have implemented these ideas and developed these habits the most quickly and the most effectively did it with a small group of friends who supported each other *and held each other accountable*. I'll have more to say about this later, but if you really want to shift the odds of success in your favor *quickly*, this is the easiest way to do it.

Let's get started.

Set Up Your Tools

I will discuss mechanics—tools, planning, making decisions, dealing with change—using a paper-based, do-it-yourself system as our platform. It does not really matter what tools you use, as long as they meet certain minimum requirements. You'll understand these requirements as I work through the basic tools and how to use them. I use a paper-based model here not only because I am convinced that paper is better for a college student (and I'll make that case in more detail later), but also because it is much easier to illustrate concepts with paper. I can avoid having to discuss every idea within the peculiarities of every available electronic option.

I'll fully discuss paper vs. electronic later. For now, paper is simpler and easier.

You will need the following supplies:

- a 50–sheet pad of 8-1/2" x 11", 1/4" ruled graph paper,

- a supply of 3" x 5" index cards; a package of 500 will see you through a semester,

- a supply of letter-size, 1/3 tab cut manilla file folders; a box of 50 will last at least a semester,

- something with which to label file folders; as cheap or as extravagant as you want to get,

- a file drawer in a desk or cardboard letter file storage box (sometimes called a "banker's box"),

- optionally, a 1/2" 3-ring binder, and a 12" ruler.

Total cost for the minimum, mandatory kit is about $15. If you spend more than $25, you're going overboard.

Set up your calendar. You will use two facing pages of graph paper to lay out a calendar for one week. Figure 1 is a model of what you will want. You'll need enough weekly pages to span the length of your term or semester. You want enough to cover an entire grading period.

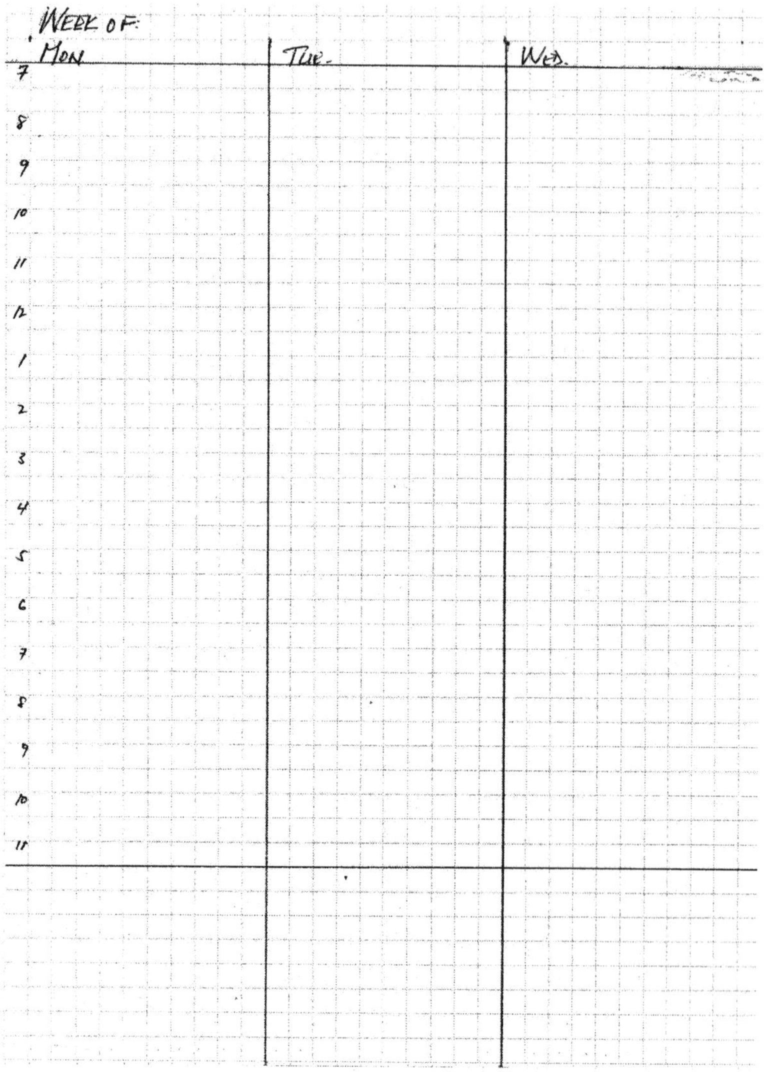

Figure 1: The left–hand–side of the weekly calendar. Nothing fancy. Note the tickler space at the bottom of each day.

On the left hand page, create columns for Monday, Tuesday, and Wednesday, as shown. "Week of: " goes in the upper left corner. Leave about two inches at the bottom margin; this is "tickler" space. On the left margin, write in the hours of the day. If you think you'll have early morning commitments (club meetings, workouts, etc.) then start the day as early as necessary, *but no later than 8 AM*. Use two rows per hour. You should have enough room to get to 8 PM; don't worry if you can't go much later than that.

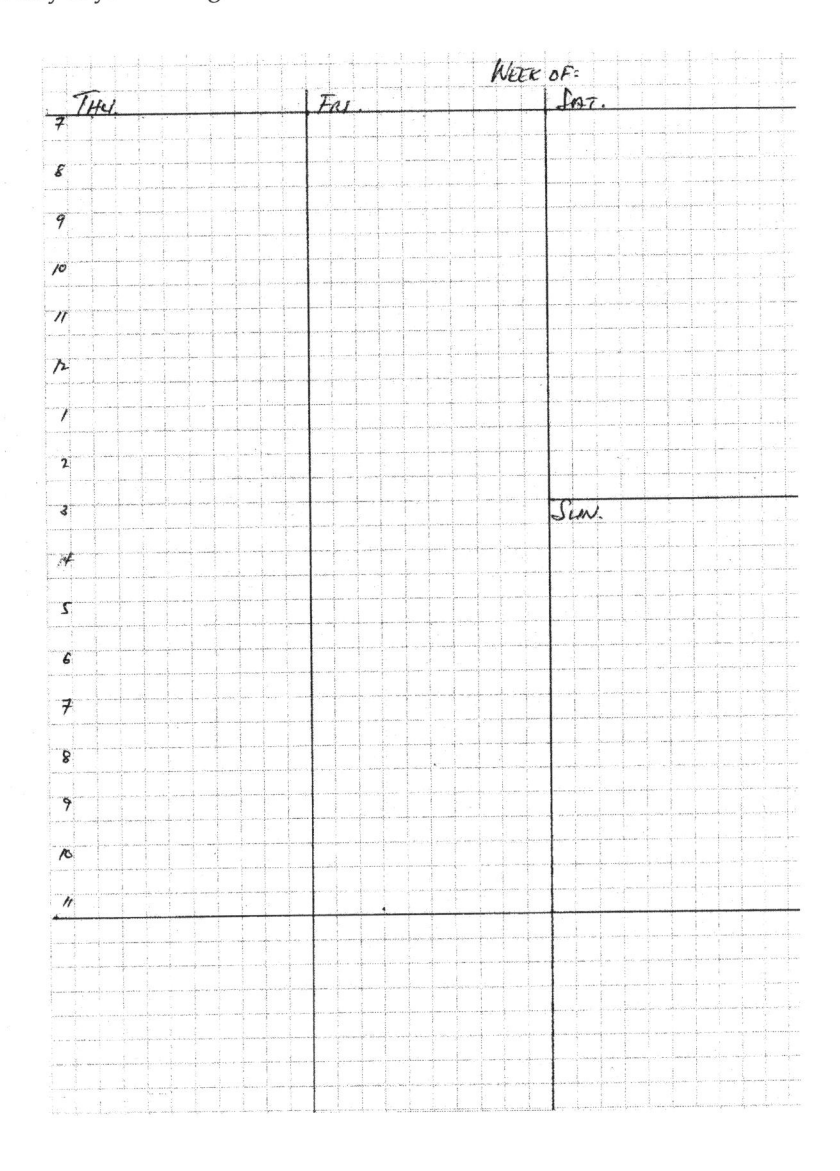

Figure 2: The right–hand–side of the weekly calendar. Tickler space at the bottom. Don't worry about labeling hours of the day for Saturday and Sunday; just pencil them in as you need them.

The right hand page is similar, except that the third column will be used for Saturday and Sunday and doesn't need a separate time-of-day line. Do enter the hours on the left margin; you'll use these for Thursday and Friday. Add the same amount of tickler space at the bottom. "Week of: " goes in the upper right corner.

Make an original for the left and right sides, then photocopy as much as you need. If you can get the photocopier to make duplex copies you can save a little paper, but don't waste time—if you do everything single-sided you'll only need thirty pages or so to cover an entire semester.

Once you have enough pages for the semester, fill in the dates. Punch the sheets and put them in the three-ring binder, or simply put them in a file folder. Get this done *quickly*; do not waste time pursuing perfection.

If you're not inclined to make up your own, there are several pre-printed calendars available. Some are better than others. The important features are:

- column layout for each day of the week;

- a column wide enough so you can actually write enough meaningful info in a given time slot;

- a small amount of blank space, either attached to each day or a separate space for the whole week—this is "tickler" space; a place for reminders of things that must be done on a specific day but don't have a specific time associated with them;

- a long-enough day—too many have an hour range that covers only the typical 8–5 workday; you'll need more than that;

- the pages *do not* give up a lot of space to extensive to-do lists, expenses, notes, mileage, or other unnecessary categories of distraction.

You want a lot of calendar space, a small amount of tickler space, and nothing else. It's the calendar space that matters, so you want as much real estate for this as you can get. If your school gives you a planner, calendar, or agenda and it doesn't meet these specs, don't use it. Make or get your own.

There are too many products available to give specific recommendations; you'll have to look at them and decide for yourself. The advantage to buying one off-the-shelf is that you save yourself a little time. The disadvantages are the expense (some of these can cost $30 and up) and that most of them cover a calendar year, not an academic year, so you end up with some waste when you get started.

Another alternative is a wire-bound computation notebook. These run a little larger (about 9-3/8" x 11-3/4") and are graph ruled, with heavy, high quality paper. Wire-bound lets it will lay flat on the desk when opened. These notebooks have 152 pages; one notebook is good for five semesters. They can be had from online sources for $17–$22.

The only downside is that because you can't remove the pages you have to draw the entire calendar layout yourself. If you go this route, do a semester at a time. When I tried this, I found that after laying out the first few weeks meticulously, I could eyeball the layout from there. This solution will give you something of better quality without the expense of a pre-printed solution, at the expense of a little more of your time.

The only pre-printed calendar I would recommend with any confidence is the Moleskine A4 Ledger Weekly Planner. This comes as close to the ideal layout as I have seen. Well-made, good quality paper, expensive, and follows a calendar year. If you like and can afford good tools and want to save some time, it's a good option.

There's not much to say about index cards. Buy 500 at a time. I like yellow. Manila file folders are as simple as you can get; no explanation required. If you want to be a little extravagant, get a half-dozen plastic file folders. These will be used for more permanent, on-going use, as you'll see shortly. They are extremely durable (I have some in my file drawer that are at least ten years old) and are a useful luxury.

Open a package of index cards; take out a bunch (it doesn't matter how many; grab more if you need them). Make up a few to look like the example in figure 3; I'll refer to these as "assignment cards." After you've done this twice you won't need the labels, but use the format consistently so you'll know where the relevant information is without having to do a detailed read of the entire card. Binder clip or rubber band them, and set them aside.

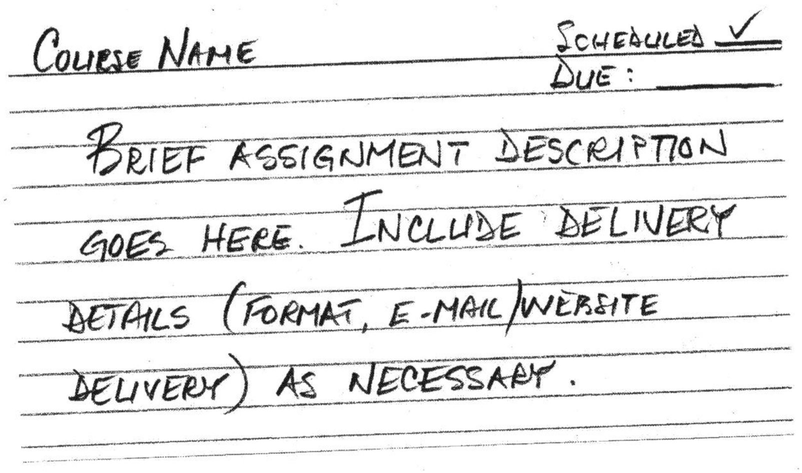

Figure 3: The Assignment Card. Keep it simple. Put just enough information on the card so you know what to deliver, how to deliver it, and when it is due. Once you've scheduled the work in your calendar, check off "Scheduled."

Take out a few file folders; one for each course. Label each one with the course name followed by "WIP" (Work in Process); e.g., "Calculus–WIP". These folders are where you will keep any paper-based work for the current assignment in that course. One per course should be sufficient, but courses with a lab component may require a second dedicated folder.

Take out another bunch of folders and label one for each course with the course name followed by "—backup"; e.g., "Calculus—backup". This is where you'll store copies of every assignment you deliver. It is also where you'll store work that is returned with a grade. These files are critically important, and we'll discuss them in more detail later.

Empty out the file drawer in your desk, if you have one, or set up the file storage box. Label the box as you wish such that a roommate does not accidentally dispose of it or move it to storage (it happens). In the file drawer or storage box, put your work-in-process files in front, followed by your backup folders, followed by the remaining unused folders.

That's it for basic setup.

The Workflow Management Process

The guiding principles:

- You have 168 hours in a week, but you have only the "whitespace" (the uncommitted time on your calendar) in which to live your life and get your work done.

- You must make *conscious* decisions as to how you will use your time, in advance, and these decisions must reflect *your* priorities.

- You must be able to trust your system to capture everything you have or want to do such that you can make effective decisions as to when and how you will do it.

- You must be able to trust your system such that once everything is captured, you can forget about it until it is time do it.

In general terms, there are three levels of planning:

- beginning of term or semester planning;
- daily, or as necessary, planning;
- weekly review planning (the most important).

We'll walk through a streamlined example of the process, and you'll see how these tie together.

Daily Plannning—Managing an Assignment from Start to Finish

There are four parts to managing an assignment:

1. Get the assignment.
2. Plan the work.
3. Do the work.
4. Make backup copies and deliver the completed assignment.

Simple enough. First, you'll get the assignment. Assignments can come to you in class, on the course syllabus, e-mail, a course website, or a social media site. The burden is on you to know from where your assignments will be coming, and to deal with them accordingly.

With an assignment in front of you, from whatever source, you'll create an assignment card (AC). The details of ACs were covered in the previous chapter. Put just enough detail in the assignment description so you are sure you understand what is being asked of you—what you have to do, what you have to deliver, and when it is due. If necessary, write a reference to the source of the assignment ("see syllabus") if there is too much detail to put on the AC easily.

If you *don't* understand the assignment well enough to write a summary description, do not wait—get help immediately. Knowing you have an assignment without knowing exactly what it is you're supposed to do or deliver causes unnecessary stress. Make an appointment, write an e-mail, catch your professor in the hallway, but do whatever it takes to get clarification as quickly as possible.

You will end up with a stack of assignment cards. Daily or "as necessary" planning starts with your stack. At the end of the day, or whenever you have ten minutes, sit down with your ACs, your calendar, a pencil, and an eraser. Go through your assignment cards, figure out when you're going to do each one, and schedule them in your calendar in available whitespace time.[1]

You will have to guess how long it will take you to get the work done. Don't worry about the accuracy of your estimates. Make your best guess quickly, schedule the assignment, and move on to the next one. As you schedule assignments, check off the "scheduled" box or space in the upper right corner of the card. Continue until all of your current ACs are scheduled.

From here, it's a simple matter of doing what your calendar tells you to do, according to the decisions you have made. If it's Tuesday at 10:00 AM and your calendar says that before your 11:00 AM class you have planned to do your Chemistry problem set—that's what you do.

It's that simple, and that hard. We'll discuss this in more detail later. We'll also discuss what to do when you don't finish an assignment in the time you have allotted. For now, we'll assume that everything goes as planned.

Your work on that assignment is done when you have finished the work, it is in the form required for delivery, and *you have made a backup copy that you have placed in the "backup" folder for that course.* Check off the "completed" box on the assignment card, and if it is a paper backup copy, staple the assignment card to it. If the assignment is being delivered electronically, make sure you have a physical

---

[1] This is "processing" your ACs, and is the connection between what you have chosen to do (ACs) and when you will do it (your calendar).

copy of the work (printed); put this in the folder along with the assignment card. You might want to make a note on the card as to where on your computer you stored your work. I would recommend that you go further: if the assignment was delivered by e-mail, print a copy of the e-mail; if submitted through a web page, either print the page or print a copy of the confirmation notice that some online course systems generate. Attach the assignment card.

Why the obsession with backups? Work gets lost. Like it or not, the burden of proof will be on you to show evidence that you completed the work on time. Students tell me this happens frequently, so be prepared.

Assuming servers don't crash, an e-mail submission will create an audit trail—you pull up the e-mail with your work attached from your "Sent Mail" folder (you did keep a copy, right?). Work delivered on paper can be a little more difficult—I don't think you'll convince your professors to "sign here" on your assignment card to acknowledge receipt of your work.[2] But if there ever is a question of whether or not you did, in fact, submit a paper-based assignment on time, your case is much stronger if you show up with your backup folder full of copies of completed assignments with delivery dates on them—including the assignment in question.

The only thing left is to deliver the assignment as required: in class, in a faculty office or mailbox, by e-mail, or through a website. You are now done—completely—with that assignment.

The sequence is simple. Assignments come in and you generate an assignment card. Periodically, but at least once per day, you process your stack of ACs by scheduling each one on your calendar. You do your work per your decisions as shown by the calendar. When you have finished the work, you create the necessary backups and deliver the work as appropriate. You can do this daily planning as often as you think necessary, but at the end of the day all of your current assignments, as represented by your stack of ACs, should be scheduled.

WHY GO TO THE TROUBLE of creating assignment cards? Why not write assignment information in the calendar?

In our approach here, the calendar reflects your *decisions* about how you will use your whitespace time. Your stack of assignment cards reflects the details of *everything you have chosen to do*.

There is nothing to prevent you from writing out assignments in the calendar. You will face two challenges: first, there is probably not enough room to write out all the details in the allotted time; secondly, odds are good that you will be re-planning regularly (much more on this later) and moving things around. Every time you make a change

[2] I had friends who were stuck with a professor so completely unorganized that they felt they had no choice but to try.

you will have to re-write the entire assignment in another time slot on the calendar.[3]

Separating decisions about time (calendar) from decisions about what to do (ACs) creates hard boundaries between parts of your system. This will make calendar entries easier; because details are on the AC you only need a summary entry in the calendar. A check mark in the upper right corner of a card will tell you whether or not that work has been scheduled, so knowing whether you have accounted for everything is just a matter of quickly flipping through the stack.

The assignment cards answer the question "What have I chosen to do?"; the calendar's job is to answer "What have I decided I will be doing now (or at some specific time in the future)?" Clear, clean, and simple.

Beginning of Term/Semester Planning

You should do this in the first few days of the semester, or as soon as you have syllabi for all your courses—whichever comes soonest. This is cheap insurance. The hour or two you spend on this will insure that you get off to a productive start at the beginning of the semester. It will also reduce the risk that some unaccounted commitment will mess up your plans at some point.

You should have your basic toolkit—calendar, index cards, WIP and backup file folders, and a place to store them. Get out your calendar, and round up every scrap of information you can get about anything happening in your life over the course of the upcoming term. This could include a school master calendar, syllabi or course descriptions, course websites, or social media. If you participate in athletics, clubs, or any other regularly scheduled non-academic pursuit, try to get the schedule of practices, meetings, and games.

Now gather up information relevant to all other time commitments you might have in the next few months. This could include family commitments, doctor or other healthcare appointments, church activities, or travel plans. If you work at a paying or volunteer job, try to get your work schedule as far in advance as possible.

Don't be surprised if the pile is quite large. There's a lot going on in your life; just how much may be a bit of a shock when you get it all in front of you. You may also have this nagging feeling that there's something else you *know* is going on at some time in the future, but you can't quite remember it right now. Do the best you can and don't worry. You're going to deal with as much as you know now.

Start filling in your calendar. Begin by entering all of your classes for the entire semester. Then add the rest of the information you

[3] More bluntly, a to-do list (or stack of ACs) unconnected to the calendar is little more than wishful thinking.

have, as far into the future as you can. Once you've added the details for academic and recurring non-academic commitments, stop for a moment and think about what other activities might make regular demands on your time. If you're commited to maintaining a regular program of exercise, schedule it now. If you have an important recurring social engagement, get it on the calendar.

Do all of this scheduling in pencil.

Your goal is to identify any and all *hard commitments* of your time. These obligations could be your choice or someone else's, but at this point it doesn't matter much. What you want is to know what these commitments are, as far into the future as possible—because what's left is the unscheduled time, or whitespace, in which you'll be able to make decisions as to how you'll get your work-life done.

As you go through this process, make a note of exam dates or any other significant deadlines; for example, simply put "exam" next to the class entry for that particular date and time. If a major assignment is due at a particular class meeting, note that in the calendar. If it is due on a particular day but not at a specific time or place, make a note in the "tickler" section of your calendar for that day ("Comp Lit research paper due").

You are done when you have stared at your calendar for ten minutes and have not added anything. Do not worry if you know that you have some commitment out there, but don't have enough information to get it into your calendar. As long as you are reasonably confident that you have the first month of the term or semester pretty well accounted for, you're fine. Put the calendar pages in their folder or binder, put the folder or binder where you'll know you'll find it—your backpack or messenger bag, desk drawer or inbox on your desk—and forget about it. You're done for now. Daily planning and weekly review planning take over from here on.

Weekly Review Planning

If your goal is to not only get your work done but also to make sure that you include important non-academic pursuits and actitivites in your life, then the weekly review is where you make that happen.

Planning once at the beginning of the semester will get you off to a good start, but is obviously not sufficient. Daily planning will help you get the work done but will leave you in a reactive mode that will make it difficult to include non-academic commitments. Stepping back at the end of one week and the beginning of the next to take a longer view gives you the opportunity not only to account for your academic obligations, but also to make sure you have scheduled time for those things that, taken together, constitute having a life.

Your goal is to cultivate the habit of managing your life in weekly blocks. This is far enough in advance that you can plan for and anticipate academic obligations without stress, and close enough to the present that you should be aware of 100% of your assignments and commitments. You'll be able to make good decisions as to how you'll get your work done, and you'll also be able to set aside time for non-academic activities that are important to you.

The foundation of any habit is consitency, so pick a time at the end of the week and set aside about an hour. Make this a hard commitment in your calendar for every week of the semester. If you're unsure when to do it, I'll recommend Sunday evening around 8:00 PM. Try not to schedule other work at this time. The benefits of the weekly review come from thinking clearly about the week ahead, and you don't want to be distracted by the stress of having to complete an assignment for Monday morning.

THE WEEKLY REVIEW PROCESS IS SIMPLE. In summary form, here's what you'll do:

1. Gather all of the "inputs" in your life—anything that may represent a potential commitment of your time—into their respective inboxes.

2. Assess the previous week: how did it go?

3. Look forward: anything coming up that could create further demands on your time?

4. Process all of your inboxes to empty.

5. Process all of your ACs—get everything on your calendar.

6. Review the calendar: reasonable? In line with your priorities?

   We'll walk through each of these in detail.

I USE "INPUT" HERE to mean anything that could represent a potential claim on your time:

- assignment cards;

- schedules for non-academic activities;

- anything else that could represent a hard time commitment for something you either have to do or want to do: a doctor's appointment, going to the gym, attending a symposium, going to a party.

These inputs could come to you through any one of several channels:

- in class
- e-mail
- phone, text, or voicemail
- a course website
- social media
- a conversation with a friend
- paper (course syllabi, regular mail, campus newspaper)

Managing inputs starts with managing channels. You can't control everything, but over time you can steer important inputs to a few channels of your choosing. If you don't manage these channels it is easy to feel overwhelmed; conversely, consciously steering important inputs into one or two channels goes a long way toward simplifying your life. There is probably not much you can do about how faculty choose to communicate with you. But you do have some control over almost everything else.

To illustrate, consider two scenarios. First, imagine what can happen if you don't manage input channels. You dutifully respond to every e-mail, Twitter tweet, Facebook status, blog posting, voicemail, etc., because it's possible that important stuff could come through any of these channels. It's almost guaranteed that something will fall through the cracks, and the necessity of having to check all of these sources is a source of stress in itself.

Consider another scenario. Your professors prefer e-mail, so you'll have to pay attention to that channel. You tell your friends and anyone else, as necessary: "I check my e-mail twice a day. That's the best way to reach me for something that is important but not urgent. If it's urgent, call me—leave voicemail if I can't answer, and I'll get back to you as quickly as I can."[4]

The second scenario reduces the number of channels from an approximate maximum of eight to a manageable two (e-mail, phone) for important communication. This doesn't mean that you'll never look at text messages or social media, but over time you'll know that if it's important, it will come to you through one of your preferred channels. Manage these channels, and the odds are good that you will have dealt with the important stuff in your life. Stress reduced.

Students I know who have tried this report that they get some initial pushback ("Why don't you answer my texts?"), but after a

[4] You might not say this in so many words nor quite so directly, but you can get the message across over time.

week or two the important stuff comes through on their preferred channels; they can ignore almost everything else. It's your time and your life, so decide what works best for you.

MANAGING INPUT CHANNELS SIMPLIFIES THINGS to some degree, but you still have to account for everything that is coming at you. You have to make sure that inputs, no matter what channel they come through, end up in the same place, consistently, so you can be confident that you have dealt with everything. You need an inbox.

It used to be that a single, physical inbox was sufficient. Regular mail arrived and landed in the inbox, which was a real box or tray in an office or a designated spot on the kitchen counter at home. Family members or co-workers might leave you a note if you missed a phone call. But now there is voicemail, text messages, and possibly social media to contend with, plus regular mail (or anything on paper) and e-mail.

Voicemail and e-mail have their own virtual inboxes, and you can get a physical inbox (or a file folder) to hold physical "stuff" until you decide to look at it (or your weekly review, whichever comes first). Text messages and social media don't have inboxes, so you need a way to funnel these inputs into one of your other inboxes.

USE INDEX CARDS to get information from other channels into your physical inbox. A few examples:

- A friend sends you a text message about an upcoming social event. It's not urgent, but you need to RSVP this week. Note the details on an index card and drop the card in your inbox. You can decide how you'll respond later.

- You're reading the school newspaper, and there is an event next week that you might want to attend. Note the details on an index card, drop it in your inbox, and make a decision at your next weekly review.

- You're having coffee with a friend. He suggests getting together with a few other friends to plan a hike. Make a note on an index card, drop it in your inbox, and make a decision at your next weekly review.

At this point, anything and everything that could possibly represent a commitment of your time has found its way to an inbox (if not, corral everything *now*). You'll get to emptying them in a moment. First, you need some perspective.

START BY ASSESSING THE PREVIOUS WEEK. Slow down, relax, and enjoy the process. This is your *life* we're talking about here.

How did your week go? Were you able to get your work done on time, have time for other important things, get enough sleep, and keep stress at a reasonable level? Did you stick to your plan, or did you occasionally fall off the wagon? Why, or why not? What can you learn about managing your work and your life from what happened?

Now look forward. Look at your calendar for the next two to three weeks. Any exams coming up? Any project deadlines? Important non-academic events that will require preparation time, or could consume time beyond what normally happens in a given week? Any random or unexpected events—family commitments, doctor's appointments? For academic tasks, create an assignment card as necessary ("study for Diff. Eq. exam," "plan Comp. Lit. term paper"). These ACs may or may not have a deliverable associated with them, but they do represent a commitment of your time. Add these to your AC stack for later scheduling.

PROCESS ALL OF YOUR INPUTS, which is just a fancy way of saying that you will go through *everything* in your various inboxes and decide whether it repesents something you have, or want, to do. The following description applies to any inbox, real or virtual. Take an input off the top of the pile:

1. Is the input important? In this context, important means that it requires some action from you. If not, and the information is nothing you'll ever need, delete it or throw it away. If no action is required but you might need this information later, save it in a "Reference" folder (*not in your inbox!*). If you know you'll need it on a specific date, make a note in the tickler section of the appropriate day.[5]

2. If the input requires action (be careful—what would be the real consequences of not doing anything?), what *specific* action is required? If you know what you have to do and it can be done quickly (1–2 minutes), do it now. Save the original input in the appropriate "Reference" folder as necessary. If you're not sure what you have to do *or* you do know but it will take more than two minutes, create an assignment card for it. Note the action required [6] and just enough additional information so that you can find the original input later (in "Reference" or some other file). Put the AC on your stack to be scheduled later.

The process is the same for all inputs, and you'll continue to process them in this fashion until all inboxes are empty. Note that nothing goes back into an inbox. Once an input comes off the pile,

[5] It's easy enough to set up a "Reference" folder in any e-mail system; since e-mail is searchable simply move the e-mail there for retrieval later. For paper, you will outgrow a single "Reference" folder pretty quickly. Use a simple alphabetical (A-Z) filing system.

[6] When you're not sure what you will have to do, your AC is going to be a request for clarification. Don't guess. If someone wants something from you, the least they can do is be clear about it. If they're not, don't waste your time until you know exactly what you're being asked to do. Then you can decide if this is important or not.

you make your decisions and either trash it, do it, or create an AC for it, and file as necessary.

ONCE EVERY INBOX IS EMPTY you will have your calendar and a stack of ACs in front of you. Now you will go through the stack, scheduling each AC, and in the process, create your life as you want it to be.

Take a minute or so—no more—and flip through the stack. You want to get a quick read on the relative priority of each task. If it helps, you can sort them into A, B, and C priorities. Don't over-think this, just satisfy yourself that you have a good idea of what the most important "stuff" is.

Start scheduling. For each AC, figure out when you're going to get it done, and enter it in your calendar (*in pencil!*). You will have to wrestle with priorities, and don't be too concerned if it doesn't all come together on the first pass. You might find that some of the "required" actions aren't so mandatory after all—delete them. Go through whatever number of passes are necessary to get everything on your calendar.

Why not go straight to the calendar as you are processing the inputs out of your various inboxes? Why bother with the intermediate step of capturing required actions on assignment cards? The presence of a required task, as captured on a card, represents a conscious decision by you to *do something*, but that's all. You now have to decide *when you will get this done*. In the process of making that decision you will have to assess the priority and importance of this action *with respect to everything else you have to do*. You can do this most effectively when everything you have to "do" is in one place—your stack of ACs—and you can make those decisions in one sitting.

I won't tell you this will always be easy. Making these decisions, especially trying to assess relative priority—is *this* more important than *that*?—is not simple, and the more you have going on in your life, the more complex it will be. But this is your opportunity to craft your life as you want it to be.

LOOK AT YOUR CALENDAR FOR THE COMING WEEK. Does it look reasonable? Does it reflect your priorities? Does it allow you to get your work done, have a little fun, and get enough exercise and sleep? Do you have time for important people in your life? If not, make changes now.

These are important questions. I'm not a big fan of the idea of "balance," because that implies an external standard as to a "correct" allocation of your time. Only you can decide upon the best combination, but decide you must. Making it a conscious decision means you can make corrections later, as necessary.

This raises an obvious problem—what happens if you run out of whitespace for things that simply must get done in the following week? It happens, and we'll discuss this in detail later. For the moment, assume everything fits. The objective is that at the end of your weekly review, your calendar should represent a reasonable plan of action for the coming week. If you have activities and studies scheduled into the wee hours every night and no whitespace anywhere, you're asking Mr. Murphy to show up and mess with your life.[7] You can't fill every minute, because life will intrude. Your plan should be reasonable without you having to be superhuman.

Give the calendar a last review and ask yourself:

- Are you doing what *you* think you should be doing? Does your calendar reflect that?

- Does your calendar reflect your priorities in all areas of your life—academic, physical, spiritual, social?

- Does your calendar reflect a path that is taking you closer to your long–term goals and the life you want for yourself?

If these questions stimulate some serious thinking, write your thoughts down on an index card and drop it in your inbox. Process it at your next weekly review. Does this thought, idea, or concern represent anything you should *do*? If so, schedule accordingly. It could be as simple as making an appointment with a professor to discuss an assignment, an on-campus job, or an internship. Knowing that you've captured these important-but-not-urgent items will further reduce stress, and contribute to a sense of having your arms around *everything* going on in your life.

All of this should not take much time. Daily planning should require no more than 10–15 minutes per day. Beginning of semester planning is a one–time, one– to two–hour session that will pay big dividends. Your weekly review should require no more than an hour. If you spend much more time than these rough guidelines, you are investing too much energy creating plans that will likely change. Most of the time, close enough is good enough. Keep it simple, and don't obsess.

Done? Put it all away and enjoy some quiet time. Then get a good night's sleep so you're ready to go Monday morning.

That's the nutshell version of the basic process. To this point we have assumed that everything has gone according to our insightful planning, we're executing the plan, getting things done, and life is great.

We'll discuss a little later about what to do when life doesn't line

[7] Murphy's Law: whatever can go wrong, will go wrong.

up with your carefully crafted plan. Right now I want to take a slight detour and address the paper-vs.-electronic question.

Do I have to use paper? Can't I use...?

No, and of course you can, subject to a few requirements.

There are two reasons why I chose to present the mechanics of planning and decision-making in the context of a paper-based system. The first is a practical one: if I had to explain these concepts in terms of the details of the most popular software applications, this part of the book could easily consume one hundred pages. That is too much space and time to devote to what is not really the most important part of the book. Paper does not require explanations of how to set up accounts or users, setting configurations, or specific techniques for how to enter or delete information. This makes it easier (and much more brief) to focus on the essential ideas without getting bogged down in trivia.

Secondly, I want you to get on with this process *quickly*. The goal is to start making conscious decisions about what you will do with your time and your life, *not* to waste a lot of it debating the pros and cons of various applications.

That said, I'm convinced that paper is better than electronic *for college students* for several reasons:

- You already know how to use paper. No FAQ required.

- You can put together a paper-based system for as little as $20. Not every college student can afford a laptop or a smartphone with a data plan.

- Paper doesn't crash, doesn't require recharging, and will not present you with a blue screen of death at inopportune moments. Backup means running your calendar pages and ACs through a copier.

- A file folder and a small stack of index cards weighs 5–6 ounces; let's say half a pound. A laptop with charging cord weighs 5-7 pounds. The paper-based system takes up less room in your backpack.

- A paper-based system is not something likely to be targeted by opportunistic thieves.

- Paper is faster, more flexible, and easier to read.

- Paper is personal. We tend to remember much better what we write than what we type.

But—and it's a very big "but"—I really don't care what physical tools you use. As you'll see, the mechanics are important, but they are not the whole story. So if paper is a deal-breaker for you, go ahead and use whatever electronic tools you want, subject to the following:

1. The calendar should allow you to see an entire week of complete days at one glance. You should not have to scroll up-down or left-right to see everything you are committed to doing that week. A full-week view makes planning and responding to change much easier than a day or partial week view. This means that your laptop screen might work if the screen is large enough. Smartphones are impractical for this level of planning and decision-making; you can force the issue but you will endure a degree of unnecessary frustration. Tablets, especially the larger ones, can be made to work, but this could be an extravagance, given that you'll need a real computer (laptop or desktop) to do real work.

2. The application-device combination should work such that there is *one* place to go to see what you should be doing right now, and *one* place to go for the details of that task.

3. If you choose to use a virtual rather than a physical inbox, make sure that a) there is only *one* inbox, and b) everything (including inputs that come in on paper) finds its way to your virtual inbox to be processed. This will likely require that you invest in a scanner. Know that the risk of overlooking something increases directly with the number of inboxes, so keep them to a minimum. You want to know that when you have processed your inbox to empty that you have accounted for *everything*.

4. Either have a regular backup strategy, or store your "stuff" in the cloud. If you are cloud-dependent, do you have multiple means of access to the Internet? If campus-wide Internet service were to go down, how will you access your system? Not a huge problem, but you want to be prepared.

5. Do *not* get sucked into exploring every possible tweak and hack for your chosen software. This is another form of procrastination. Get the important information down in the right place, and get back to work. You don't need a perfect system; you need a good-enough system that you can trust and that you use all the time.

6. If your chosen tool(s) have notification or communication/collaboration features, turn them off. Your system is your servant, not your master, and you will decide when to look at it.

7. Stick with whatever tools you have chosen for at least a semester before making changes, and do not change tools in the middle of the semester. There is no perfect system (paper, electronic, or otherwise), so don't waste time looking for it. Stick with what you have and make it work. This is a hard temptation to resist, as the blogosphere is constantly buzzing about the latest and (doubtfully) greatest personal productivity app.

Enough. Make your choice and live with it. Paper is better but you can disagree; it is more important that you pick *something* and use it consistently. Get started. The more important stuff is coming up.

Life Will Not Go as Planned

The Map is Not the Territory; or, Change is Normal

No plan of any complexity survives intact for long. Change is inevitable, and you have to develop an attitude that change is normal and expected. You must learn how to deal with it effectively and efficiently.

There are countless reasons why your plans will change:

- you underestimate how long it takes to do an assignment, so you have to find time later in your calendar to complete it;

- a social event/club meeting/athletic practice goes longer than anticipated, cutting into your planned work time;

- weather—a snowstorm shuts down the campus on the day you needed access to the library;

- you receive e-mail from a teacher changing an assignment such that you can't do it at the time you planned or in the time you allotted;

- you have to work online and the server crashes, with no indication of when it will be available;[8]

- you get sick;

- you have to deal with a personal or family emergency;

- your assignment is a group project and you need input from other group members to do your work—and they don't deliver on time;

- you're working on a long-term project and you realize that the research will require a lot more time than you originally thought.

You can certainly imagine several more examples. The end result is the same—your plan is no longer viable. The process for dealing with this situation is straightforward.

[8] With the increasing use of online course delivery, I'm hearing this complaint much more frequently now than a few years ago. Forewarned.

Re-plan as Often as Necessary

It will be obvious when your plan cannot work as it stands. Get out your calendar, a pencil, and an eraser. What can you move around to make room to get things done?

- Can you "compress" a minor assignment—make a conscious decision to do less than you might given other circumstances?

- Can you work through lunch so that you can get to bed on time?

- Can you cancel a minor social engagement, skip a club meeting, or tell your coach you can't make it to practice today? This might seem a little radical, but it's your time, so it's *your choice*.

- Can you split an assignment into a few parts that you can squeeze into blocks of whitespace that you might not have scheduled? Reading assignments can work here.

- Can you push some work off into the future to free up whitespace for work with earlier deadlines?

Re-work your plan to the point where you are confident that you can get your work done and live your life according to your priorities. Make whatever tradeoffs are required, but *decide*. Once you're satisfied that the revised plan is reasonable, your stress level will drop and you can get back to work with confidence.

Do not obsess with the search for the perfect plan. Close enough is good enough. Odds are good you'll have to make changes tomorrow or the next day, so don't waste a lot of time in pursuit of planning perfection. Get to the point where you feel better, then get to work.

Make Conscious Decisions

Notice that I have not said anything about what your priorities should be. I'm not going to tell you:

- how late you should work,

- how much effort you should put into your academic work,

- what the balance should be between your academic work and your non-academic interests.

I'm not going to tell you how to live your life. What I will tell you is that you have to consciously *tell yourself* how you're going to live your life, and those choices must be reflected in your calendar.

You will continually have to make decisions of the form "Activity A is more important than Activity B." Make these decisions without fear. There are rarely any long–term consequences for a less–than–optimal decision, and you can fix it (re–planning is nothing more than "fixing it") later. To the extent that you are willing to accept responsibility for the consequences of your decisions, you have the power to control your time and your life. You have more control than you think.

A few examples to illustrate:

- You make a conscious decision *not* to do a perfect job on assignment A so as to free up more time for assignment B, which is more important to *you*.

- You make a conscious decision to miss an athletic practice—even a game—because you *know* you need more time to prepare for an exam, and you are unwilling to be up studying until 3:00 AM.

- You make a conscious decision to re–schedule a date with your boy/girlfriend because your family is dealing with a minor emergency and could *really* use your help on Saturday night.

- You catch a nasty stomach virus that leaves you with no energy and confines you to within ten feet of a bathroom. You make a conscious decision to forego a short assignment so you can get some rest and shake it off more quickly.

All of these decisions will have consequences:

- You may not be happy with the lower grade you recieve on assignment A, which is the price you paid for doing a better job on assignment B.

- Your coach might be unhappy with your decision (to say the least) and may discipline you in some fashion. Your teammates may be disappointed in you. But you would rather deal with that than the stress of cramming for, and the resultant poor performance on, an exam that is important to your long-term goals.

- You may not get credit for the short assignment, but you're pretty sure that getting back to full health sooner will be better for your long–term academic performance than trying to gut out the work and staying sick longer.

Re–planning, then, is a process of considering alternatives, examining the potential consequences of those alternatives, and re–scheduling such that the results are consistent with *your* priorities for *your* life. Change will happen and this will cause some stress. The best way to deal with change is to confront it directly. Make your decisions and re-work the plan until you have something you can live with, even if this means accepting some short-term pain. Odds are good that your decisions will result in a plan that maximizes your gains and minimizes your losses to the greatest extent possible, given the circumstances. That is more than good enough, and will enable you to get back to work with confidence.

Although it sounds like a lot of work, re-planning is about the equivalent of daily or as-necessary planning, so ten to fifteen minutes should be enough.

Make your decisions, re-work your plan, and don't look back. *Do not hestitate*. If you have any doubts about the workability of your new plan, fix it. You might have days where you have to do this more than once. Don't waste time or energy worrying about it. Re-plan as often as necessary until you like what you see on your calendar.

You now have the tools and the basic skills to handle just about anything that comes along, either in your personal life or your academic life. But there are a few special situations that occur often enough that it makes sense to know how to handle them ahead of time.

How to Dig Yourself Out of a Hole

This happens to everyone sooner or later. The common cause is extended procrastination—you got off track, experienced a few weeks of minor depression, put off (or just ignored) a bunch of work—and now you have three weeks before finals to pull your posterior out of the fire. If you don't, the consequences may be frightful to consider.

It's also possible that you're in a hole for reasons fully out of your control:

- A serious illness kept you out of class for an extended period.

- There was a death in the family (unfortunately, it happens, and death doesn't care about your calendar or how much work you have to do).

- A major administrative screw-up prevents you from going to class.

- Your professor radically changes assignments, exam dates, or deadlines just a few weeks before the end of the semester.

If procrastination is the cause, spend a little time trying to learn from the experience. Don't beat yourself up overly much, just replay events in your mind and try to figure out where you could have made better decisions, what might have happened to tempt you into poor ones, and how you can do better in the future. If the cause is related to events truly out of your control, then you have to muddle through as best you can, but you might have a few options. Talk to your faculty as soon as possible. There may be some room for negotiation as to what, and how much, work you have to do. But don't wait.

Either way, take a deep breath, tell yourself with confidence that you will deal with the situation, and get on with it.

YOU KNOW YOU'RE IN A HOLE. As the saying goes, stop digging. Do *not* lay in a store of caffeinated energy drinks and think you'll function on no sleep for the next three weeks. It doesn't work. Yes, you can do it, but you won't like the results. Instead, you're going to take an hour and do a slightly modified form of the weekly review. At the end, you'll have a reasonable plan to get you through the end of the semester without being up until 3:00 AM every night.

First, gather up everything: ACs, your calendar, syllabi, your inbox, and everything else that might represent a commitment of time between now and the end of the semester (including the final exam schedule, if you can get it). Make sure your calendar is up-to-date with all of your academic commitments: classes, labs, group meetings, etc. Now is *not* the time to skip classes. Pencil in your non-academic commitments. The goal is the same as any other planning session—you want to start with an objective picture of the whitespace you have in which to get the work done.

Make a list of:

- all outstanding assignments between now and the end of the semester,

- exams, what they will cover, and their date; and,

- *force-rank them* in order of priority, highest to lowest. Don't spend too long; you simply want a clear picture of what is truly important, versus what is nice but not critical.

Decide how much stress you are willing to tolerate. If you know you can't function on less than seven hours sleep, then set a hard limit on the end of your day for 11:00 PM. If you're willing to push a little (and I don't recommend more than this), then extend your day slightly, either in the morning, or evening, or both, but make sure that these are hard limits in your calendar.

The early bird strategy. College students are reluctant to start their day before 9:00 AM, if that early. Before blowing off the possibility of being productive earlier in the day, consider this: a friend of mine dug himself out of a serious hole (very serious, and not his doing) by adding two hours to the *beginning* of his day. He would be up at 6:00 AM, grab a muffin and a cup of coffee at the dining hall, and be working by 6:30. He would work until 8:30, then get another muffin and coffee before heading off to a 9:00 AM class. He told me that he accomplished more in those two hours in the morning than he ever did between 10:00 PM and midnight.

The only "secret" in his method was that he made sure he was in bed by midnight without fail. He told me that as long as he got six hours of sleep every weeknight (a little more on weekends), ate enough, and got a little exercise, he could maintain that pace for a few weeks. He noted that study spaces—the Student Center, out-of-the-way locations on campus—were *very* quiet early in the morning, so he was rarely interrupted or distracted.

I tried his method when I was in graduate school (out of necessity, if not quite panic). It required about three days to adjust, but was otherwise painless. Getting an early start had as its reward a productive day that ended at a reasonable hour. Before dismissing this strategy out-of-hand, think about how it might work for you.

YOU HAVE A CLEAR PICTURE of the depth of the hole you're in, and how much whitespace you have, at the moment, to work with. Now you must make some hard decisions about your non-academic commitments. You want to free up as much time as possible. Be ruthless; if things work out a little better than anticipated you can always add them back later. For now, free up as much time as you can.

Go back to your list of outstanding assignments and exams, and start scheduling them from most important to least important. Allow adequate time for exam preparation, and far enough in advance so as to keep a lid on your stress level. If you can get everything done by extending your day a little and crossing off a few social activities, then (a) the hole was not too deep; (b) count yourself lucky, and (c) get to work.

If you run out of whitespace before you run out of work, be of stout heart and good cheer. You simply need to make some decisions about what is important, what is less so, and be willing to live with the consequences.

You have two paths to consider:

- You can reduce the *number* of assignments you'll complete before the end of the semester (choosing from those that will have the least impact on your performance), thereby freeing up time for more important work.

- You can reduce the *time* you spend on some assignments, thereby freeing up time for more important work, at the risk of delivering a lower-quality product on low priority assignments.

Your decisions will likely reflect a combination of these strategies. Look for the combination that will allow you to deliver the optimal amount and quality of work in the time you have. A few examples:

- If you have a class that has a lot of regular homework assignments that don't contribute overly much weight to your final grade, you may choose not to do them (especially if you're otherwise in good shape in that class) so as to free up time for more important work.

- You may be willing to suffer a lower grade on a major project if that allows you to get it done more quickly, thereby freeing up time for other work—especially if the project is in a class unimportant to your major.

- Depending on your grade going into the end of the semester, you may—if possible—make the strategic decision to do the minimum amount of work required, live with the grade you will get, and focus on other work. This is a little risky; confirm your grade assumptions with your instructor before making this decision. But it can pay off if it frees up a lot of time. This opportunity most often presents itself in classes where the final exam is optional.

Keep cycling through your assignments and your calendar, making decisions until you arrive at a plan that meets your requirements:

- the grades you want;

- the level of stress you are willing to tolerate;

- how much of your non-academic interests you are willing to sacrifice for the short-term.

You will know you are done when you look at the plan and start thinking that it looks reasonable. *Do not* expect perfection; if your hole is deep, the outcome will not—cannot—be perfect. But the outcome will be a lot better than if you had tried to manage it all by the seat of your pants with a lot of caffeine. Instead, know that when your plan approaches reasonable, your stress level will come down, and you will have made the best of a bad situation.

Get to work. You can survive anything for three weeks.

With a little luck and the dedicated application of the skills we've discussed, you'll never have to do this. But I recommend going through a less-stressful version of this exercise at your weekly review with three weeks to go in the semester. Knowing exactly how you're going to finish your remaining work, deal with finals, and wrap up all the usual extra end-of-semester stuff will reduce stress, reduce the likelihood of nasty surprises, and give you the confidence to wind up the semester without burning yourself out.

Project Work

Some assignments require more than one task to produce the deliverable. This is especially true of writing assignments, which will require reading and research, analysis, and then writing. The writing itself may require several steps: an outline, several drafts, and a final draft. Lab reports and programming projects would qualify as writing assignments under this definition, and have similar characteristics.

Multiple steps make it more difficult to make accurate estimates as to the time required to get the work done. This uncertainty causes stress, because it is related to risk. Projects are risky on two dimensions:

- You may, or may not, know all of the tasks required to complete the project;

- For the tasks you know you may, or may not, have a good idea as to their time requirements.

Risk can change over time. You might start research for a project, only to find after your first few readings that your work has to head off in a completely different direction, thus requiring still more research and readings. You might get halfway into a programming project and realize that your current design will not handle a certain requirement efficiently, and it will take far too much time to force the design to accomodate that requirement—thus requiring you to step back and re-work the design. Somtimes you get lucky; after the first few tasks you have a clear picture of the remaining work, and all that remains is to grind it out.

For our purposes here we'll define anything that has more than one task associated with the deliverable as a project.[9] Successfully managing project work requires that you accept that projects are inherently risky due to their uncertainty with respect to the tasks involved and the time required. The goal, then, is to actively manage this risk.

Project assignments come to you through all the normal channels. Like any other assignment, your first priority is to make sure you understand what you are being asked to do, and what you are expected to deliver. Now create an Assignment Card for the project, with a

[9] David Allen. *Getting Things Done: The Art of Stress-Free Productivity*. Penguin Group, New York, 2001

few minor differences. The front of the card stays the same. On the back of the card, list the first two, three, or four tasks that you'll have to do. Do not worry about the accuracy or completeness of the list, other than the first task. Try to make these tasks of a size that you can complete in one work session, as you would define it. *Schedule the first task as soon as possible.*

Now take a minute (no more) to assess the risk involved with this project. Is it fairly low, like a lab report—are you pretty sure of the steps involved and how long they will take? Is it moderate, like a programming project, where analysis and debugging time are unpredictable? Is it high—a loosely defined research project? Conscious awareness of the risk involved will help you make better planning and scheduling decisions.[10]

Do the first task. Then look at the task list on the back of your AC (this would happen as part of your daily planning). Given what you know now, does the task list need to be changed? If so, do it now, concentrating most heavily on *the next task*, and schedule it as soon as possible.

Repeat this cycle until the project is complete—with one modification.

The standard advice from teachers, counselors, etc., for major project work is "get it done early." The standard approach of most students is to put it off as long as possbile, for very good psychological reasons—doing it early means pain now for a very distant reward; we tend to act when action and reward are more closely linked. Neither strategy works well.

The student strategy back-loads stress on the end of the semester, when workloads and stress tend to peak. The result is a lot of late nights, no sleep, and burnout.

The "wise mentor" strategy front-loads stress unnecessarily. Hustling to get a project done early involves taking time away from other work, and this may not be a good idea. Professors tend to overlook the fact that you have work in other courses. We need a strategy that will allow you to manage the risk of a project such that you get the project done, your other work done, and live your life, all at minimal stress and according to your priorities.

You manage risk on a project by front-loading the work to the point where you are confident of both (a) the tasks that remain, and (b) how long it will take to get them done. After you are sure of the remaining tasks and the time they will require, you can schedule them as you see fit to blend in with your other commitments and still get it all done on time. The benefit of this approach is it returns control of decisions affecting your time and work back to *you*.

This means that every time you complete a task, stop for a mo-

[10] Risk is not the same as how much weight a specific assignment contributes to your final grade. A low-risk project could still be a large percentage of your final grade.

ment and assess risk. If uncertainty remains high, schedule and get the next task done as soon as possible. If you think you have reached a point where uncertainty is largely eliminated, then schedule the next task as best fits with all the other things you have to do.

Projects go bad due to failure to manage risk or delaying the start of the project until you have backed yourself into a corner. Everything has to go right the first time, and when it does not, then come late nights, stress, poor work and missed deadlines. Time is also lost from a failure to confidently identify the next task and getting after it, which results in a lot of "wheel spinning" and re-work. All can be avoided with the process just described.

Major projects—those that require several weeks, or an entire term or semester—require a little more administrative support to allow you to keep track of everything. For these projects it is unlikely that the complete task list is going to fit on the back of an index card. In this case, use the assignment card only to keep track of the status of the next task. Create a file folder for the project. For a really large project, this will be a "master" folder. Inside the front cover, staple a sheet of paper. This will be your project task list, and you should have enough space on a single sheet to keep a detailed list. Again, the focus is on the *next* task, and the list will change—so do it in pencil. Review and change as necessary, but at least at every weekly review. Do not be afraid to make wholesale changes as the project goes on. *The next task is always found on the Assignment Card.*

Major projects may require multiple storage locations for the work-in-process. You might have paper resources in several file folders, files on your computer, files on a school computer or server, or work-in-process on a course website. You want *one* place to begin looking for any and all of it. Staple another sheet of paper on the inside of the back cover of the master project folder, and title it "References". On this sheet, add a pointer to the location of every project resource. This takes seconds, but on large projects, it can save all kinds of wasted time trying to remember where everything is.

Regardless of the size of the project, the management process is the same: focus on repeatedly getting the next task done until your are comfortably certain of the remaining tasks and the time they will require. Then schedule them as you would any other assignment.

Managing Group Work

Group work is a nuisance. It takes enough discipline to make your own decisions about work and time, and now you have to coordinate these with other people, all of whom might have very different priorities and work habits. Unfortunately, the trend is toward more group work rather than less, so you need to deal with it.

Group work is inherently project work[11] (more than one task) or you would not need a group to get it done. As part of your assessment of the risk of the project, try to ascertain the level of commitment of your team members. I repeatedly hear horror stories of group work that degenerates into a set of people who do the work, and a set of freeloaders who are only along for the ride. Depending on your professor's policies, you may or may not be able to fire freeloaders. If it is going to be a problem, better to be aware of it early on.

The simplest scenario is a group project that is really just individual work that gets collated into a final deliverable. You know what needs to be done, in what order, roughly how long it will take, and you have the resources you need. Divide and conquer. Use assignment cards to make sure everyone knows their part, their deadline, and their deliverable.

Group projects get hard to manage when they are more like high risk individual projects—you are uncertain about the actual tasks, the time required, or both. You manage the same way—focus on accomplishing early tasks quickly so that you get to the point of certainty (with respect to tasks and time requirements) as quickly as possible. Then you can divide and conquer.

A few comments:

- No matter what the risk level of the project, try to front–load the work to the extent you can. This will tell you very quickly if everyone is going to pull their weight, or if you'll have to deal with a freeloader or two.

- Never assume that you can work up until a deadline. Someone will drop the ball at some point, and possibly for a good reason. Life intrudes. Leave yourself some slack in your group schedule to recover, if neceesary, before the deadline. The riskier the project, the more slack you need.

- It is critical that at the end of every meeting everyone understands what their next task is, when it is due, what they will have to deliver, and the date and time of the next meeting. Do not end a meeting without everyone being clear on this. Group work has enough headaches without having to deal with "...but I didn't know we were having a meeting!"

[11] Group work carries additional risk when you consider that a chunk of your GPA is now dependent upon the quality of work done by others.

Summary

1. Life rarely goes according to plan. The key to the success of your life/work management is not how well you plan, but how well

(and how often) you re-plan.

2. Digging yourself out of a hole is re–planning on a bigger scale. You can change the number of assignments you will do, the quality of the assignments you will do, or both. Decide how much stress you're willing to tolerate, and eliminate as many non–academic commitments as possible to free up whitespace for your work. Decide which classes and assignments are important, and which are less so. Make your decisions and re-work your plan until it looks reasonable, then get to work. You can survive anything for three weeks.

3. Projects are assignments that require more than one task. Your focus must be on executing the *next task* as quickly as possible, repeatedly, until you are confident of the remaining tasks and the time they will require. Then you can schedule the remaining work as you see fit.

4. Group work is project work with other people, which makes it messy. Use assignment cards to manage people and tasks. Front-loading the next task is your best risk reduction strategy. There are no sure-fire techniques for dealing with your team members (and their own challenges and priorities) so plan and muddle through the best you can.

Procrastination, Work Ethic, and Winning the Internal Game

To this point we have focused on mechanics—the tools you'll need, what to do, and how to do it. We looked at how to make conscious decisions about how to use whitespace time so as to have a reasonable plan for work and life. We examined the idea that this planning should reflect your priorities, and it should also be readily amenable to change when life intrudes.

If it were this simple, we could end the book here. Planning is important, but if you have wrestled with these issues, you know that it takes more than just making entries on a piece of paper to make it all work.

If most of your academic success is predicated on getting the work done, then most of getting the work done is related to the strength of your work ethic. Work when it is time to work, play when it is time to play, keep each in its proper place, and the results—likely favorable —will take care of themselves.

If it is this simple, why is this so hard? Why is procrastination such a problem?

I have to assume that you understand that academic success requires work—real work, and a lot of it—and you are willing to do it. I further assume that you are basically happy, or at least satisfied, with your school and program of study.

We are hard–wired, to a degree, to procrastinate. We are most strongly motivated to act *now* when action is closely followed in time by reward or pleasure or the immediate avoidance of pain. When we complete our academic work, our reward is potentially distant in time. It may be weeks before we get an assignment or exam back, and end-of-semester grades may be months away. It is easy to trivialize the reward for any single assignment, and we convince ourselves that the pain of poor performance is not important ("I'll make it up on the final..."). This separation between performance and reward, the perception that the reward on any given assignment is not significant, and the trivialization of pain for poor performance all add up to a situation that practically begs for procrastination.

The act of planning creates its own problem. Planning, calendars, and any other influence to "do it now" are interpreted as a loss of freedom of choice—and we push back:

- "I don't want a planner telling me what to do..."
- "I like to keep my options open..."
- "It's more fun to be spontaneous; I don't know what I'm going to feel like doing, so planning makes no sense..."

All of these are indications of either an inability, or an unwillingness, to make a hard decision about what to do with time. Procrastination is the consequence.

The irony of the situation is often lost. In the interest of flexibility and keeping options open, students choose not to make a decision. The decision, by default, is to do nothing. This goes on until all of their freedom is gone, because it is 3:00 AM and that major project is due that day—and there is no choice but to accept the stress and try to salvage the situation as best they can.

Work Ethic Defined

Ask a few of your friends: "How strong is your work ethic?" You'll get puzzled looks and defensive answers. If they don't change the subject, they might offer as evidence their latest all-night work session where they skipped meals and the essentials of personal hygiene, and pumped a lot of caffeine to meeet a deadline.

They would be correct to some extent—under the pressure of an imminent deadline, they finished *something*. They did not roll over and quit, and there is merit in this. But is this really evidence of a strong work ethic? Or is it really evidence of a continuous habit of procrastination? *A self-perception of a strong work ethic combined with repeated late nights and lost sleep is not evidence of a work ethic that is really working*. We need a better definition.

Our approach to managing work and life is to have complete awareness of what we have to do, and to make conscious decisions as to how and when we will get it done. In this context, work ethic becomes a measure of our consistency in the moment of decision—when the calendar says work, do we work? The more often we can answer that question with a confident "yes," the more we have a genuinely positive work ethic. When the answer is "no," we are procrastinating, with the inevitable negative consequences.

Procrastination is devious. We can rationalize any particular instance until we back ourselves into a corner. Then we rise to the occasion. The work may get done, but it's not our best and the stress is not fun.

Let this cycle repeat itself a few times, and we find ourselves in a hole of our own digging. We ended up in this predicament not because of any major event, but through a series of small (and poor) choices—death by a thousand cuts. It can happen a lot of ways:

- Your professor returns an exam, one that you prepared for thoroughly and thought you had executed well. The grade is disappointing, almost depressing. You have a two-hour work session planned after class to work on a project for that course, but your bad mood causes you to blow it off in favor of commiserating with friends.

- You did not eat well yesterday and slept poorly last night. Your energy level is low, and your emotional state matches it. You were supposed to make significant progress on research for a term paper that counts for a large percentage of your grade in an important course. Instead, you spend most of the afternoon playing video games.

- It has been a long winter. The first hint of spring arrives and that afternoon the campus has magically transformed into a semi–tropical paradise. The afternoon of work you planned is lost to a pickup softball game.

- You are hidden away in a secluded section of the library in the early evening, making good progress on a major project that is important to you as well as to your grade in the course. Friends find you and invite you to join them for pizza and Monday Night Football. You pack up, thinking you can return to the work later that night.

- You have two hours to get through a terribly boring assignment due later today. The work is not hard, but there is a lot of it and you have no particular love for the subject. Your laptop is open on your desk, and a social media chat notification chimes—a friend wants your attention. An hour later you are wondering how you will get the rest of the work done in time.

None of these are significant in isolation. The payoff for the choice to procrastinate is a lot more immediate than the reward for doing the work. But string several of these decisions together, and you have a good start on digging yourself into a hole. Recovery will require late nights, lost sleep, and unnecessary stress, all of which you are trying to avoid.

Procrastination's cause can be internal—a poor physical or emotional state, or external—friends, random events like an unexpected change in the weather, or technology. How can we prevent it, or at least minimize it?

We can stack the deck in our favor by:

- reinforcing the planning habit,

- strengthening our work ethic, and

- managing interruptions.

Reinforcing the Planning Habit

The more you use and work your system—keep your ACs updated, make changes to your calendar as necessary, look at your calendar frequently, and be consistent with your weekly review—the more you will tip towards making the right decision in the moment. Your calendar is a contract you make with yourself, and consistency—that our actions match our words and self-image—is a powerful psychological trigger. Over time, such behavior becomes more habitual than conscious, and thus reduces still further the likelihood of succumbing to procrastination.

How do you form the habit, especially if all of this is new? If you have never done anything like this, the prospect can be daunting. The psychology literature is full of research on how we form habits and how best to do it—commitment contracts, implementation intentions, etc., and they can be made to work. But they are also time-consuming and complex. We need a couple of simple, direct approaches.

Use your system. Do it continually throughout the day. In the morning you might look at your calendar to see what you will be doing and making sure you have what you need to get it done. In the afternoon, update your ACs and modify your calendar as necessary. In the evening, do a summary review, make sure everything has been captured in your system, and sleep well knowing that you are ready for tomorrow.

This is a good start, but maintaining this behavior over time can be really hard. *Get help*. Set up a system of accountability—a feedback loop—by working with a few friends or a trusted adult/mentor whose job it is to keep you on track. This is powerful. Find a few friends willing to try to develop these habits and work to support each other. You are, in a sense, drawing on each other's reserves of will power, and my experience has been that this is truly a case of the whole being greater than the sum of the parts.

Get your group together. I think three is ideal, but if you are more of an extrovert and like bigger groups, go ahead—just make sure the group stays focused. Introverts will do better with smaller groups and tightly focused meetings—you can even script them, if it helps. Choose your group carefully.

You have to agree to meet frequently. In the early days, every day is not too much. From there it can go to every two to three days, and when you reach the advanced stage, once a week. The job of the group is to ask each member:

- Did you *consciously* plan your work and your life?

- Did you do what your calendar said to do, when it said to do it?

- If not, why not?

Meetings should be short; for three people 15 minutes should be enough. Lunch or dinner meetings work well. The goal is positive reinforcement and honest feedback. If someone falls off the wagon, spend a few minutes examining why, what they might do to get back on, and how to prevent it in the future. Remind each other that it's your time and your life, and you want to be the one in control of it.

I am convinced that group support is the most effective thing you can do to grow these habits and make them stick.

Make The Right Decision in The Moment

This sounds good in the abstract—plan, work when it is time to work, make changes as necessary. So how is it that we get derailed? In our hypothetical examples above it was never some significant or calamitous event that causes procrastination. It was simply *a poor choice in the moment of decision*. The way to avoid these small moments of weakness is a simple ritual: STOP—BREATHE—LOOK (at your calendar)—THINK.

The psychology literature is full of research that concludes that our primary decision-making strategy is to make quick decisions and snap judgements. This was a survival skill early on, but is not so good for our purposes. The ritual is just a simple, direct way to interrupt the automatic response long enough to allow you to *pay attention* to your decision-making process.

Let's look again at our hypothetical scenarios and consider some alternative endings:

- You are justifiably upset at your unexpectedly poor grade on an exam. Class has ended, and your lousy mood is making you seriously consider blowing off your planned work session. *Stop*. Be still. *Breathe*. 10 seconds is plenty. Let the emotions flow through you. *Look* at your calendar—what do you have planned, and if you don't do it now, how will you get it done? What will be the consequences of procrastination? *Think*. Do you have options? How annoyed are you, really? It is one exam; there will be more. Could you move your planned work session to another time without undue stress? Can you take 20 minutes for coffee, and then get to work (at least you'll get *something* done)? Can you move assignments around so you can work on something more interesting for the next two hours? Make the right decision.

- Your physical state is poor for any number of good reasons. Your plan calls for a lengthy block of time to be spent doing research for a term project, but your motivation matches your physical state. You are sorely tempted to do almost anything else. *Stop* and *breathe*. Be fully aware of how you feel without judging it, one way or the other—just notice it for a moment. *Look* at your calendar. You really don't have the energy for an intense work session, and forcing the issue might be a waste of time. What can you move around? Do you have a reading assignment you could get done in some quiet space, with little energy but with the help of some good coffee? Can you move some other work around and make it a point to get to bed a little early tonight? *Think*. Realize that you have options. Make the right decision.

- Your friends find your hiding place in the library, and want you to join them for pizza and Monday Night Football; about 2-1/2 hours. You are making good progress on an important assignment. You know the process. The important difference is that this time the source of potential procrastination is external. Your friends matter. But anytime *anyone* wants to make demands on your time, your automatic response must be "wait a minute...let me look at my calendar." This buys you the time you need to go through the ritual and make the right decision.

- You are working away and your laptop beeps. A friend wants to start a chat session. Go through the ritual, and make the right decision. But there are important aspects of this scenario that deserve further exploration.

Technology, Interruptions, and the Distracted Brain

It is fashionable to bash social media and cellphone technology (except, perhaps, real phone calls) as wasteful of our time and attention. It's a minor media event when a celebrity hipster announces an "Internet sabbatical." These technologies promote and reward a broad, shallow, and superficial use of our brains, with corresponding effects on our interpersonal relationships.

I'm ambivalent. I don't want to tell you how, or even whether, you should use text messaging, social media, e-mail, IM chat, etc. My concern, for our purposes here, is that every technology, for all the hyped advantages, usually comes with a cost. The common theme running through everything we have discussed is *conscious choice*—to be fully aware of all you have and want to do, to make conscious decisions about priorities, and to put these together in the form of an objective plan (subject to change). If these technologies carry a potential cost that could negatively affect your ability to do these things, then you need to be aware and develop ways to deal with it.

I'll define "technology" as the landscape of all computer, Internet, and cellphone devices and software applications. They overlap, and the functionality of the technology is changing every day, but this will work for now.

The common feature of all of these is the ability to notify, communicate, share, or collaborate, with the power to do so *initially vested in the sender*. This is no different from the telephone and postal mail when they were the dominant means of communication, but both of them had limitations. Regular mail is delivered once per day, six days per week. Landline phone service was limited by social norms; calling an office phone was limited to regular business hours on weekdays, and it was considered rude to call someone at home after 9:00PM. If we were not in our home or office, we were unreachable and not subject to interruption.

Contrast this with today. The almost-everywhere, all-the-time availability of the Internet and cellphone technology is multiplied by the number of technology-based channels: e-mail, several flavors of social media, text messaging, IM chat on several platforms, video chat with conferencing capabilities—the list goes on.

The beginning of the downside of these technologies is that we use them with the behavioral norms with which we used to manage regular mail and landline phone service: when the phone rings, we answer it; when the mail lands on the desk or kitchen table, we open it. The problem is that now we have several "phones," and they are ringing all the time.

One example is sufficient. A Pew Research Center study looked only at text message use.[12] The median number of text messages received by members of the 18–24 demographic is 50 per day. The cost of interruptions is not only the time for the interruption itself, but the time it takes to get back, fully focused, on what you were doing before you were interrupted. Assume each message costs three minutes, start to finish. Let's further assume that the messages come in at a steady pace between 9:00 AM and 9:00 PM, which means

[12] Aaron Smith. Americans and text messaging, 2011. URL http://pewinternet.org/Reports/2011/Cell-Phone-Texting-2011.aspx

about four an hour. At this rate, you would be losing 12 minutes of productive time per hour, 2-1/3 hours of time for the whole day, or roughly 20% of your available time.[13]

I'll leave it to your imagination to assess the combined effect of text messaging, e-mail, and the many forms of social media. The *potential* problem is obvious: we have created an environment where we can be interrupted by anyone, anywhere, at any time. Unmanaged, we will have ceded control of a very large part of our time and attention, which are the two dearest possessions of any college student.

If you want to be consciously in control of your time, attention, and your life, then you will have to make some decisions as to which channels you will use, and when and how often you will grant them access to you. Earlier, we discussed the idea of limiting access for important communication to two channels. We used phone and e-mail in the example, but the choice of the channels is up to you. Start by thinking about through which channels comes *important information*.

Important means information that would require action on your part, or perhaps require you to change your plans—your choices are limited, and you will have to do something, now or in the future. Look at the channels that can currently reach you, and mentally rank them as to their "importance quotient."

Different students have different experiences. Most of those with whom I have discussed this (and passionate discussions they were) eventually converge on e-mail as the source of the most important information—stuff they could not ignore. Pressing further, there was some agreement that important information came through phone calls, regardless of whether they actually had a conversation or picked up the information from voice mail. From here, opinions differed. Social media and text messages were a gray area—either could be the channel through which a study group coordinated meetings, but that information came at a cost of having to filter out a lot of ignorable noise to get to the important stuff.

You'll have to make your own choices, but in the interest of getting you started quickly, try this: check e-mail twice a day at whatever hour is most convenient for you. If there is something that requires action from you, either do it immediately, or make yourself an assignment card to prompt you to deal with it later. *Turn off all notifications*. Use the phone for urgent stuff. Ignore everything else.

This sounds extreme (no texts?! no Facebook?!), and it is, by design. Try it for a few weeks and see what happens. Your friends may wonder why your are not *immediately* responding to their text messages, but they'll figure it out. See where the really important

[13] The inescapable conclusion from this research is that we spend an awful lot of time interrupting each other—and this study only deals with text messaging. Add the effects of e-mail and social media for yourself. Text messaging has its uses, but I'm now a little more aware of whether or not my critical message is really important to my intended recipient *before* I hit "send."

stuff is coming from, and manage accordingly.

Why spend so much time on this? Constant interruption takes control of your time and attention away from you, and it really messes with your ability to learn.

Working Memory, Attention, and Learning

Short-term memory is where all input from your five senses is first processed. Most of these inputs are filtered out unless the data represent a survival issue, and a good thing, or we would be constantly distracted. Long-term memory is more than just storage; your mind takes what you learn and associates it in new patterns with existing knowledge. The more this recombination effect happens, through repetition and more learning, the stronger the long-term memory. It is this recombination that constitutes, for all practical purposes, *learning*.

Your working memory is a subset of short-term memory. Working memory is the sum of those inputs *to which we pay attention. It is our consciousness in any given moment*. It is our life, as we are experiencing it, right now. The capacity of working memory is small. Since the late 1950's researchers assumed five to seven items, plus or minus two, as the limits on working memory capacity. Recent research has revealed that this overstates the case by a factor of two—we are limited to 2–4 items in working memory,[14] and this limit is remarkably consistent across individuals.

[14] John Sweller. *Instructional Design in Technical Areas.* PCS Data Processing, Inc., New York, 1999

Working memory is where all learning starts. Information has to go into working memory and stay there for some time before the process of creating long-term memory—new knowledge—can begin. This is where interruptions do all their damage.

The limited capacity of working memory implies that when our attention shifts, a new item moves into working memory. This means that something that was already there was bumped out. If the item that was bumped was what we were trying to work on, work with, or learn, then we have to stop, refocus our attention, and get it back.

Learning is dependent on moving information out of working memory and into long-term memory. This process is dependent on *attentiveness*, which is a mental process, and *consolidation*, which is a physical process that begins building new proteins and chemical pathways in your brain. These two processes, when they work together, begin the changes by which new information is combined with existing knowledge in new patterns. This is how we learn, and this is how we build long-term memories.[15]

It takes about an hour in working memory before your brain starts the process of consolidation. During that time, three different regions

[15] Nicholas Carr. *The Shallows: What the Internet Is Doing to Our Brains.* W. W. Norton & Company, New York, 2010

of your brain form and open up new biochemical pathways so as to move knowledge around and begin the process of associating new knowledge with existing memories. The complexity of this process makes it fragile. [16]

This biochemical process is facilitated, or hindered, by the strength of our attentiveness. Attentiveness is precisely defined in this context. It is the sum of the strength of our concentration and the intensity of our intellectual and emotional engagement with what we are trying to learn. The stronger our attentiveness, the more directly the consolidation process takes place.

We pay a price, in terms of our ability to learn, when we have to deal with constant interruptions. The price is paid two ways. The first is cognitive overload, and the second is increased "switching costs."

Working memory capacity is limited. Interruptions force new data into working memory, which means we will rapidly fill, and overload, that capacity. This can put us in a constant loop of having to get back to what it was that we were trying to focus on, because if it's not in working memory, we will never learn it. This is cognitive overload.

Switching costs are the price we pay in time, energy, and delayed learning as a consequence of cognitive overload. When something we want to work with gets bumped from working memory, we have to stop, find it, put it back, and build up the engagement (intellectual and emotional) that constitutes a state of powerful attentiveness that is most conducive to the consolidation process. Research concludes that switching costs can last up to twenty minutes between interruption and the time it takes to become fully attentive to what we were working on previously.[17] This has obvious consequences with respect to our ability to get work done.

To summarize, then: Interruptions undermine our attentiveness, which is the strength of our engagement with the contents of our working memory, by inducing cognitive overload. When cognitive overload is combined with the negative effects of switching costs, the quality of our attentiveness suffers and the consolidation process never gets started. It takes us far longer to get our work done than necessary, and we don't learn much in the process.[18]

Decide for yourself how best to manage it. The simplest and quickest way to start is to turn off all notifications, and make frequent use of the silent mode on your phone. *But decide, or the technology and its interruptions will manage you.*

[16] Nicholas Carr. *The Shallows: What the Internet Is Doing to Our Brains.* W. W. Norton & Company, New York, 2010

[17] Nicholas Carr. *The Shallows: What the Internet Is Doing to Our Brains.* W. W. Norton & Company, New York, 2010

[18] Mr. Carr's work presents compelling arguments that would be easy to interpret as anti-technology. This would be inaccurate. He concludes not that technology is bad, but that how we interact with information has a direct effect on brain physiology, which affects how (and how well) we think. Worth a read; decide for yourself.

The Reality of the Student Job

The Job Description

Write a job description for "college student."

How would you write it? What skills, tasks, and responsibilities would you include?

How close do you think it would be to the perception of the job that most students have?

You probably have had a part-time or summer job. You knew, or learned quickly, that when you were on the job your employer expected you to be focused on the work you were being paid to do. It is unlikely you would go to work with the *expectation* that you could spend a significant part of your working day surfing the 'Net or Facebook, playing video games, or hanging out with friends over coffee.

In theory, a student goes to college to pursue mastery of a body of knowledge. Yet student behavior would lead an observer to think that their real responsibilities really were 'Net surfing, playing video games, or drinking coffee (or more interesting libations). You likely know this from your own experience. How often during the middle of "working hours" do you see students spending time on *anything* but work?

College faculty work to a different set of assumptions. If you have chosen to be a full-time undergraduate student, they expect your commitment to be *full*-time, and that means a lot more than the standard 40 hours per week.

This is not to say that recreation is unimportant. But faculty assume that your first priority is your studies, and recreational activities are secondary. At the risk of stereotyping, *based on observations of behavior*, the priorities of many (most?) students are reversed.

Is this overly harsh? Perhaps, and if you're reading this, your priorities are likely more in line with reality. The extremes are contrasted to make a point—*how would the quality of your academic life be different if you fully embraced the idea that as a college student, your full–time "job" is the work required of your studies?*

Confronted with this possibility, most students imagine a life of continual grind; a never-ending progression of days sitting in classrooms or hunched over books. But given the previous discussion, this is unrealistic. Good planning and a solid work ethic (as defined here) makes sufficient time for important non-academic activities and recreation.

So again—how would your life be different if you fully embraced your student "job?" More importantly, what does that mean?

It means you make the conscious decision to "go pro."

Go Pro

The tools, the system, the "hack" part of our discussion is simple stuff. A little thought, some trial and error, and you could figure this out for yourself. My goal was to try to save you the time that comes with error.

The hard part is the internal game. I am convinced that success at the internal game has nothing to do with any "nature vs. nurture" factors. It is a choice. Habits of positive virtue can be developed by anyone willing to put in the effort. It's not easy, and it is a project that never ends.

There will be days when you are a productivity ninja; a Zen master of self-discipline who gets the work done while in a state of imperturbable equilibrium. There will also be days when you will be a poster child for sloth. There will be days when you attack each work session, and days when you will sit and stare at a book for twenty minutes before doing anything. There will be weeks where your planning and actions mesh in perfect harmony. There will be weeks where your system derails completely.

It does not matter.

Steven Pressfield is a successful writer (*The Legend of Baggar Vance, Gates of Fire*) who struggled for decades to achieve success at his craft. He wrote a fascinating and short book on what he learned about the process of being successful as an artist.[19] It is his defintion of an artist that makes the book relevant. He sees an artist as anyone who pursues any goal that requires the endurance of short–term pain for the sake of long–term gain.

Given that an undergraduate college career is a four–year commitment, we can call it "long–term gain." Given also that there will be a lot of work, some of it very hard and not all of it pleasant, we can label the process as "short–term pain." We can learn a few things by adapting some of his ideas to the realities of student life.

Pressfield conquered his procrastination demons by making them real. Part of his reason for creating the idea of "Resistance" with a

[19] Steven Pressfield. *The War of Art*. Grand Central Publishing, New York, 2002

capital 'R' is to personify procrastination; to make it less abstract and more concrete. He sees Resistance as a dragon that he must slay every day if he is to continue to be successful. If Pressfield wins today, he knows that the dragon will be back again tomorrow morning to do everything possible to prevent him from doing his work. This battle is fought by every artist (his definition). Most lose.[20]

But we are not powerless. We have weapons to bring to bear, which we have discussed. We also have spirit. Pressfield defines this spirit, this state of mind, in his exhortation to "go pro."

He defines the pro as an ideal—someone who is fully committed to his vocation. "Fully" in this context means both total in mind and full-time in effort. In Pressfield's mind anything less is an amateur, and Resistance loves to mess with amateurs. Adapting his ideas we can identify the characteristics of the pro student:

- **The pro shows up—every day**. When the calendar says it is time to go to class, the pro goes to class. When the calendar says it's time to work, the pro does the work. No excuses. The class can be boring, the work long and tedious. It makes no difference. The pro does it because that's his job.

- **The pro stays on the job for as long as it takes or the calendar requires**. If the pro is struggling with temptation, he struggles, but he keeps on working. He does not quit. A pro shows up on time and puts in a full day. The pro does not look for reasons to quit, or to skip out on work or classes.

- **The pro is committed to the long haul**. College is the early days on the path toward building your adult life. This is a marathon, not a sprint. The pro works at building new habits of planning and working, and actively develops the necessary character muscles. This takes time. If Resistance wins a round, the pro does not beat himself up over it. He does not whine. He re-plans, suits up for the next round, and gets back in the game.

- **A pro masters the fundamentals of his discipline**. Every body of knowledge, every art, craft, sport, science, business, or profession has its foundational skills. The pro masters them. In an academic setting they may not be obvious. Ask your faculty. Work on these skills, over and over, until they are as natural as breathing. It will likely be dull and boring. The pro does this because he knows that this is the shortest path to mastery.

- **A pro maintains a sense of humor**. There is no guarantee that your faultless planning and indomitable spirit will prevent life

[20] Mr. Pressfield has paid his dues, and that alone makes the book worth reading. It is wonderfully brief. Some may find his concepts a little mystical; he does this to make the abstract concrete, and thus easier to deal with. When I have published as much as he has then I'll have earned the right to criticize his metaphysics; in the meantime, I can learn from him.

from messing with you. Life will intrude, plans will go off the rails, and work will suck. It happens. The pro learns to laugh at it. The pro also learns to forgive himself, when necessary, and try again.

- **A pro accepts the judgment of the real world, and knows it is not personal**. You will not always get the results you want. Faculty will judge your work by their standards, not yours, and their judgment may not agree with your perception. This is reality. The pro accepts that reality as feedback; a single data point related to performance at a single point in time. Good or bad, the pro knows that it is neither indicative of potential, nor is it personal. The pro does not get overly excited about an A, nor does he get depressed about a C (or worse). The pro learns from the feedback as best he can, and then gets back to work.

Note that these characteristics, the essence of the pro, require no special intelligence. It is a choice. You are a pro from the moment you decide to be one and start acting like one. The pro spirit is available to anyone willing to commit fully to their work. When you make conscious decisions as to what is important, how you will use your time, and then act on those decisions, you are halfway there.

This scares the hell out of a lot of people, including working adults. If these assumptions hold, then I have stripped away every excuse you have for not designing and living the life you want. For some people, this is more than they can handle. They need to be able to blame someone else for the results in their lives, so they never fully commit. The idea that they might have some influence on their life and destiny scares the pants off of them.

For others (and for you, I hope) this can be liberating. Know that you can pursue your calling as a student as you define it. You will not always be perfect, but you will know how to recover. You will improve. When you turn pro, you know that over time your successes will dwarf your setbacks.

You have allies in this imaginary war (with apologies to Pressfield, who would refer to it as anything but imaginary). Some of you can draw on resources from religious faith. Pressfield composed his own prayer to the Muses—nine Greek goddesses that were the personification of knowledge and the arts—and he recites it, out loud, every time he sits down to work. Given his success I am not inclined to be critical. Whatever works.

Good friends are your best allies. Good friends will keep you focused and remind you, when you need it, why you are here. They can be your Muse–in–the–moment: "... weren't you supposed to be working on that design project?" A trusted professor or other adult can fill the same role. Cherish them.

Know that persistence and real work trump genius, and showing up every day trumps motivation. You are not guaranteed success. But at the end of the day, when you have "showed up" and done the work required of you, when you can string those days together over a week, a semester, a year, a degree program, a lifetime, the results will take care of themselves.

Get to work.

For Advanced Practitioners

"Advanced" does not mean "harder." The ideas that follow will allow you to take advantage of the basic concepts more fully, more effectively, and more efficiently.

Set Your Schedule on Automatic Pilot

To the greatest extent possible, set up your schedule so that you are doing the same thing at the same time on the same day. Make it as predictable as you can.

Willpower is not unlimited. It is like a bank account, and every exercise of self-discipline (such as deciding to not give in to procrastination) makes a withdrawal. Make enough withdrawals and you could find yourself blindsided by procrastination later in the day, without really knowing how it happened.[21]

Fixing your schedule—"it's Monday morning, so at 10:00 AM I know I'm working on my Organic Chemistry homework..."—means you don't have to make these little decisions. After a few weeks the activity will become automatic, and you will do it without conscious thought. This leaves your willpower bank account intact, allowing you to make better decisions when you really need to.[22] The automatic schedule also makes it easier to keep up with important non-academic activities: exercise, errands, laundry, and other personal business. You can batch some of these and do them all at once; e.g., Saturday morning you do your laundry, run your errands, and pay your bills.

This is not new. In a letter to his adopted grandson, George Washington wrote: "System in all things should be aimed at; for in execution, it renders every thing more easy." Technology has changed, but what we have to do, and how we decide to do it, has changed very little over the centuries.[23,24]

[21] M. Muraven, D.M. Tice, and R.F. Baumeister. Self-control as limited resource: Regulatory depletion patterns. *Journal of Personality and Social Psychology*, 74:774–789, 1998

[22] Prof. Baumeister and his colleagues show that willpower has a biochemical component, in addition to being a character trait. Understanding the biochemistry makes it easier to develop the virtue.

[23] William J. Bennett, editor. *Our Sacred Honor: Words of Advice from the Founders in Stories, Letters, Poems, and Speeches.* Simon and Schuster, New York, 1997

[24] Everything old is new again. Our predecessors knew as much, or more, about the key ingredients of productive living when working after dark meant lighting candles.

Make Full Use of Your Daylight Hours

Tour any college campus, and you will discover a powerful cultural norm: daylight is for sleeping, going to class (maybe), eating, and socializing. The work "day," for most students, starts around 10:00 PM. Why is this norm so pervasive?

It certainly does nothing to make life better. You are up all night trying to get things done so you have to sleep as late as your schedule will allow. This upsets your internal clock so you are going at half speed for the day. You do not get as much done for the simple reason that human beings are not naturally wired to be productive between midnight and 4:00 AM. Less productive means you get less done, so you are up until 2:00 AM *again* trying to keep up. This can be a hard cycle to break. Living like this for an entire semester is no fun.

Let's challenge the norm and see what we can learn. Imagine a student with a 15 credit–hour course load. We will assume that these are "normal" courses—no lab component—to keep the math simple. A 15 credit-hour load will require 15 hours of class time per week. This could be three times a week for an hour, or twice a week for an hour and a half (or worse, once a week for three hours, which is just wrong).

The rule of thumb is that you will spend three hours working outside of class for every hour you spend in class. There are 45 hours available to us on Monday through Friday between 8:00 AM and 5:00 PM. Deducting the 15 hours spent in class leaves us 30 hours per week with which to get our work done. Assuming we make full use of that time, we need to find 15 more hours to get our work done each week. This could mean three hours per night after dinner, Monday through Friday. More realistically, we skip Friday night and do this work on Saturday, or otherwise spread it over the weekend. Do not leave it all for Sunday night, because that is your time for your weekly review—and there is little sense in injecting that stress into the start of a new week.

There are some weaknesses in this argument. Work loads are not always level; mid-terms and finals will force you to make changes in your schedule. That the example is not perfect is not the point. The point is that there are, even within a fairly demanding course load, plenty of hours available with which to get a large chunk of work done *during the day.*

Given this, having to work until 2:00 AM should be the exception rather than the rule. When I hear stories of continuous late nights and all-nighters, I suspect a lack of work ethic first, and an overwhelming course load second. I have yet to encounter a student who could make a convincing case that supports the existing cultural norm of sleep during the day, work all night.

There are challenges. Your class schedule will likely leave you with irregular blocks of time between classes. This is where planning, especially the weekly review, can really help. Try to fit the work to be done to the time available in each block as best you can. Your estimates of how much time assignments will take will not be perfect. Do not worry if you can't get everything done in the time allotted; some progress is always better than none. Avoid over-scheduling—too much work for too little time—because all that will do is leave you frustrated. Simply use larger blocks of time for more demanding work, and schedule less intensive tasks that can be easily started/stopped for shorter blocks. As always, keep it simple.

Schedule Sleep

Make a conscious decision as to how much sleep you need and what time you will be in bed each night. Put your bed time in your calendar, and stick to it. When you know your day will end at 11:00 PM, you are much more likely to get your work done during the day.

Do Not Let Roommates Dictate Sleep or Work Schedules

Come to terms with roommates. You will need to make expectations clear. It should not be difficult to agree on "quiet and dark" hours so you can sleep. If roommates want to listen to music or play video games late at night, headphones are mandatory and screens can be dimmed and pointed away from where you are sleeping. The challenge is toughest in dorm rooms where you are sharing the same physical space, but you must confront the issue.

If roommates are uncooperative, talk to your RA, the Student Housing office, or whomever, but get this resolved. If none of this works, move. This is a problem and a level of stress you do not need and should not tolerate. This will take persistence.

Why make such a big deal of this? Sleep—how much you get, and when you get it—is every bit as important as what you do during the day, for the simple reason that sleep is what allows you to function. Do not skimp on it.

Hold a Few Hours per Week in Reserve

It is tempting to fill in every minute of whitespace in the calendar with *something*. I learned the hard way that this is just asking for life to mess with you.

Workloads are not level; some weeks will be more intense than others. Stress increases when we base our fixed, automatic-pilot schedule on an imaginary level work load. We need to reserve a little production capacity for those weeks where we need some "overtime" to get everything done. We also don't want to do this overtime at 2:00 AM. Pencil in time—a hard commitment—for a phantom class. You can make it either three days a week for an hour a day, or twice a week for an hour and a half. Experiment; as the semester or term unfolds it will be obvious which makes more sense. This is built-in float, or slack, in your schedule; time that you can use to handle the demands of a more intensive week without rendering the rest of your plan unworkable.

If you don't need that time on a particular day for meeting imminent deadlines, use it to get started on early preparation for projects, exams, etc. It does not have to be intense; the whole point of building some float into your schedule is to reduce stress. Using this time during the week to get a jump on work towards deadlines farther in the future will make life down the road much less stressful.

Credit for this idea goes to Cal Newport at the Study Hacks blog.[25] It's a good idea. Imagine the benefits of studying for midterms beginning in the second week of the semester—you get to the exam date, and you really don't have to study because you are already prepared. The preparation wasn't stressful because you did it in little chunks of time spread out over several weeks.[26]

Let's deal with a logical objection—not having time to fit this into your schedule. You might not have time—or think you don't have time—to create this phantom course because either (a) you are taking too many courses, or (b) you are involved in a lot of extracurricular academic activities. Let's deal with (b) first. Take a hard look at the benefit you are getting from each non-academic activity, and compare that to the benefits that would accrue if you could be prepared for exams, projects, etc., well in advance. Weigh the benefits carefully and make an informed decision as to which one better serves you and the life you want.

The first one—(a)—is tougher. Think hard before committing to 18 or more credit hours per semester. I understand that there may be financial motivations—scholarships are good only for a limited number of semesters or academic years, and you have to get the credits required to graduate within that time. Given the ever-rising cost of college, I'm sympathetic. But keep in mind that you also want to *learn* something. If your calendar is so loaded that you can not make time for a phantom course, consider that you might be taking too many courses.

[25] Cal Newport, Ph.D. The study hacks blog, 2011. URL http://www.calnewport.com

[26] Mr. (now Professor) Newport ruthlessly breaks down the usual assumptions about academic work, skewering a few sacred cows along the way. He has a contrarian opinion about the relationship between passion and work that will make you think. Read the blog for his ideas on automatic schedules, hard focus, and being constantly aware of how you are using your time.

Use Assignment Cards as Extended Memory

All of the books ever written on time management encourage the keeping of to-do lists. The reasoning is sound. We have more to do than we can keep in our heads, so write it down and then forget about it. This frees our minds to focus on the work in front of us until we next look at the list.

This is fine, up to a point—that point being the fine line between disgorging your brain onto paper as necessary, or procrastinating by writing, re-writing, and re-writing lists. This is why I don't like lists kept in the calendar—too much time is wasted copying them from one page to the next.

Use index cards to remember non-academic tasks. My wife thinks I use index cards to remember everything. We discussed this when we walked through the weekly review process. The "life on index cards" idea is close to the "Hipster PDA" concept popularized by Merlin Mann of the 43 Folders blog.[27]

The stack can get large. Cull your stack frequently—tasks tend to get written down in all sincerity in the moment, but the passage of time shows that they are not all that important. If the task comes with a deadline, it goes on the calendar.

[27] http://www.43folders.com Mr. Mann wrote the blog for a few years, then decided he was wasting too much time writing about every trick, hack, and system for managing time. His final message was to get rid of all the toys and software and get to work.

Focus and Concentration: the Pomodoro Technique

I love this idea. So simple, effective, does not require expensive gear, and is easily adaptable to different situations.[28] I will give you just enough detail to get your started.[29]

Maintaining focus and concentrating solely on the work in front of you is hard. The Internet makes it harder. It is no surprise, then, that a lot of students I talk to tell me they have trouble staying focused for any length of time.

The Pomodoro Technique treats the ability to concentrate like a muscle. Start small, add small increments, and over time you build up your strength. Get yourself a cheap mechanical kitchen timer. You could use your cellphone, but the act of winding the timer and the ticking sound act as triggers to put you in the right frame of mind. Get set up in a location where the timer will not disturb anyone (especially when it goes off).

Set the timer for 15 minutes. For that 15 minutes, you will focus solely and entirely on the work in front of you. Not only will you not permit outside interruptions, but also you will not distract yourself—no checking e-mail, social media, getting up to stretch, going to bathroom (you should do that before you get started), nothing. Just work, quietly focused, for 15 minutes.

[28] Francesco Cirillo. The pomodoro technique, 2006. URL http://www.pomodorotechniqe.com

[29] If you want more detail, download the PDF and read the first half. Read the second half only if you are interested in his thoughts as to the psychological motivations behind focus and concentration.

When the timer goes off, set it for 5 minutes. This is break time. Get up, stretch, move. When the timer goes off, sit down, set it for 15 minutes and get back to work. After four "pomodoros" (work sessions) take a slightly longer break; maybe 10 or 15 minutes. Then set the timer for another session and get back to work again.

Keep two things in mind:

- When you are in a "pomodoro," don't worry about any other work or what you have to do next. Empty your mind completely except for what is required to focus on the work in front of you.

- *Do not let breaks expand*. When the timer goes off at the end of a break, reset it and get back to work.

The combination of the short time interval and the focus on only what you are doing for that 15 minutes sets up a situation where you begin to think "...well, I can concentrate on anything for 15 minutes..." Since a break is only 15 minutes away, there is a manageable time between now and your "reward" for working. Slowly increase the work interval up to 25 minutes. Maintain the five-minute break. Take a 15 minute break after four pomodoros. At this level you are working 50 out of every 60 minutes per hour. That's respectable productivity, and the scheduled breaks make it feel less intense.

My timer is a cheap ($3) plastic contraption that looks like a piece of garlic. Depending on the work I am doing, I may choose not to use the timer at all. At other times, when I am feeling only marginally motivated—or strongly unmotivated—I will set the timer to whatever interval will allow me to get started. This is critical. The reality of most of the work we have to do, no matter how distasteful we imagine it to be, is never that bad once we get started. I'll set the timer to a reasonable interval and tell myself that I can survive anything for, say, 10 minutes. Once under way, keeping up the momentum is easy.

You can adjust the length of the work interval to match your energy level, your enthusiasm for the work, and how much time you have. If you are tired and it is work you loathe, start with a short interval. If you get going and it is not so bad, you can lengthen the work interval. Just be aware that shorter intervals will incur more switching costs.

I have heard of some students who have successfully used the Pomodoro Technique when working in groups. The work/break sequence prevents the group meeting from breaking down into one extended social occasion where an hour (or more) goes by and nothing gets done.

Never Work in the Space Where You Sleep

Get out of your dorm room. Do not expect to get any serious work done there. Your dorm is for sleep and matters of personal hygiene.

I have had many conversations with college freshman home for the Christmas break, and I hear stories about how hard it is to get work done. When I ask where they study, they inevitably say that they try to do their work in their dorm room. Surprisingly, few get the idea to go somewhere else.

You need to find a space that has minimal noise, adequate desk or table space with a good chair, and good lighting. When working during the day, try to find a space with good natural light but not next to a window—it's too easy to lose too much time enjoying the view.

Environment has a significant effect on our productivity, and I encourage you to go to great lengths to find and set up a space that works for you. Get creative. Explore the unused spaces of lab buildings, campus office spaces, administration buildings. Get to know janitors and the crew in the physical plant department and ask them how you might get access to a space. A polite conversation with a departmental administrative assistant might get you a key to a small, unused—and private—office.

Experiment. Different types of work might require a different environment; e.g., crunching numbers for a lab report is best done in a space with different characteristics from that which would lend itself to deep, focused reading. Sometimes a change of scenery can be a good thing. Maybe there is a good coffee shop that is quiet enough that would be a good place to focus on work that requires intense creativity. Graduate students may find that a good pub is a source of inspiration. Mix it up.

When you do find those spaces that work for you, don't tell anyone.

Meditation

Meditation is nothing more than a technique and a practice for slowing down our minds long enough to silence the background mental chatter. This allows us to turn our attention to what is happening in the present moment, fully and completely.

The significant benefits of the practice are lost in the noise of Eastern mysticism and New Age spirituality. These include an enhanced ability to live in the present unworried about the past or future, the ability to calmly embrace what is happening in the moment without emotional attachment, and a means by which we can turn off the background noise in our minds when it threatens to become overwhelming.

Continued practice will increase your ability to slow your mind down long enough to focus on the work in front of you. This means that you improve your attentiveness, which is a critical prerequisite to real learning and the building of new knowledge within long-term memory.

For a more complete treatment, read *Wherever You Go, There You Are: Mindfulness Meditation in Everyday Life* by Jon Kabat-Zinn.[30] We'll cover just the basics, very simply, as an introduction.[31]

1. Find a space reasonably free of distractions.

2. Sit comfortably erect—back straight, shoulders comfortably back and down (not tense, not slouching), head comfortably erect. You can sit in a chair with your feet on the floor, or cross-legged on the floor, or in the Japanese *seiza* position with shins on the floor and buttocks on your heels. Be comfortable, but not too comfortable—you should have to expend a little energy to maintain good posture.

3. Put your hands in your lap or any other convenient place that is not a distraction.

4. Let your eyes relax. You can let them close halfway, or fully—try it either or both ways, and choose whichever works best for you.

5. Inhale fully but comfortably through your nose. Focus your attention on your breathing. Feel the air enter and fill your lungs; listen to the sound. Pause for just a moment, then exhale slowly and steadily. Keep your attention focused on your breathing. At the end of your exhale, pause for just a moment, and begin again.

6. Your mind will wander. Random thoughts will intrude on your attentiveness, and they will conspire to prevent you from becoming fully mindful of your breathing. Do not let this frustrate or annoy you. Acknowledge the thought, and return your attention to your breathing.

7. Try to "sit" for ten minutes. It will seem like a very long time; your limbs and joints might complain, your lower back will not enjoy maintaining good posture without moving for this long. Persist.

With more practice, lengthen the session. Opinions vary; some argue for longer sessions, others say that the benefits accrue in shorter sessions and longer sits are more for bragging rights than anything

---

[30] Jon Kabat-Zinn. *Wherever You Go, There You Are: Mindfulness Meditation in Everyday Life.* Hyperion, New York, 1994

[31] Every book on meditation is needlessly complex. Dr. Kabat-Zinn works hard to be complete without verbosity, and still needs 316 pages to do the job. Read the first few chapters, then dip into the remaining chapters as your interest dictates.

else. Experiment with longer sits, just to see what it feels like. You will become uncomfortable; try to acknowledge the discomfort and return your attention to your breathing. When you get to the point where you can sit for twenty minutes without too much strain, that is probably sufficient.

Although I can offer no objective evidence, my experience has been that two shorter sits—and you can define "short" however you like—is better than one longer session. It is a positive way to begin and end the day.

This is a long-term project; don't expect instant benefits. Keep up your practice, and try to apply the meditative approach during the day, in moments of decision. If you recognize the *Stop—Breathe—Look—Think* ritual as a shortened version of meditative practice, you're right. It allows you to be fully aware of yourself, your thoughts, and your emotions in the moment, giving you time to think clearly before you make a decision. Use this also in those moments when motivation is lagging, the willpower bank account is drained, and your brain is being exceptionally creative at giving you all kinds of reasons why you should not do the work you have planned right now.

Practice.

Do It Now

This is so simple. This is so hard. This is so effective.

- Your plan is in place. Your day starts, per your plan, when the alarm goes off at 7:00 AM. Do not hit the snooze button (worst thing ever invented). Get up. Do it now.

- You have showered, dressed, and had some breakfast. Your plan says you are to go to the library and finish your Calculus problem set before your 10:00 AM class. It is blowing snow and 20°F outside. Do it now.

- You have twenty minutes before your next class, which is enough time to get over to the Financial Aid office and correct some errors on your work/study application—errors which are preventing you from starting your part-time job. It is out of your way and you will have to hustle to get to class on time. Do it now.

- You have finished your last class of the day, which included a particularly grueling exam. You are mentally and physically drained. Your calendar has you scheduled to hit the gym, but the last thing you want to do right now is lift heavy objects or pound the treadmill for five miles. Do it now.

This is old wisdom. Thomas Jefferson, in his *A Decalogue of Canons for Observation in Practical Life*, written in 1825 for the benefit of the son of a friend, put this at the top of the list:

- 1. Never put off until tomorrow what you can do today.

Timeless wisdom too often ignored. Interestingly, he also added:

- 7. Nothing is troublesome that we do willingly.

which says something about the role our attitude—which we choose—has to play.[32]

The Book of Proverbs in the Old Testament is conservatively estimated as 2,500 years old. It has, by my count, at least a dozen exhortations in favor of industry and against idleness. Jefferson again, in a letter to his fourteen-year-old daughter: *"Determine never to be idle. No person will have occasion to complain of the want of time, who never loses any. It is wonderful how much may be done, if we are always doing."*[33]

This is not a life "hack" pulled off the Internet. It is wisdom—knowledge that can improve our lives—that has been around for a very long time. It would be easy to dismiss as "old school," but that would be a logical fallacy—it is not wrong simply because it is old. Consider how cultivating this attitude, in parallel with the *Stop—Breathe—Look—Think* ritual, might change your decision–making and the quality of the results you get in your life.

[32] William J. Bennett, editor. *Our Sacred Honor: Words of Advice from the Founders in Stories, Letters, Poems, and Speeches.* Simon and Schuster, New York, 1997

[33] William J. Bennett, editor. *Our Sacred Honor: Words of Advice from the Founders in Stories, Letters, Poems, and Speeches.* Simon and Schuster, New York, 1997

A Few Warnings, a Little Advice, and A Lot of Encouragement

Technology Is Not Always Your Friend

We discussed how the interruption potential of computer and Internet technologies wreak havoc with the formation of long–term memories. Controlling interruptions, by itself, will give you a significant improvement in your ability to manage your working memory, and consequently, your ability to learn. There is more.

The Internet physically affects our brains.[34] We used to think that our brains, past a certain age, were hard–wired; the circuitry was soldered in place and there was little we could do to change it. Recent research concludes that our brains are much more plastic, much more moldable, than we used to think. More importantly, how we take in information causes our brain to make physical changes so as to optimize itself for that method of information intake.

Look at whatever you think is a "typical" web page. Note how visually busy it is. The first decision your brain has to make is where your eyes should start. If the page is designed with users in mind, it will first guide your eye toward the main body of text, then toward the primary navigation section. If it is poorly designed, you will spend time and brain cycles looking around, lighting briefly in a series of locations on the page. At each visual jump (or "saccade"), your eyes pause while your brain takes what you are looking at into working memory. You make a quick decision as to whether or not that link, video, image, button, text box, or whatever, is what you are looking for. If so, you click or do what is required. If not, the eye–search starts again.

After some experience, this process becomes so natural that we are totally unaware of it. We might get frustrated with a web page so poorly designed that we cannot find what we need no matter how much our eyes bounce around the screen. The bigger problem is what is happening inside our brains.

Taking in information from the Internet through web pages re-

[34] Nicholas Carr. *The Shallows: What the Internet Is Doing to Our Brains*. W. W. Norton & Company, New York, 2010

quires the ability to scan quickly and make many rapid decisions as we search for what we want. When we do this long enough, our brains start to re-wire themselves internally to become better at this process. This is fine by itself—we are more adaptable than we think. But we pay a price when our goal is deep learning.

The Internet builds a brain physiology that maximizes our ability to deal with information in a superficial, shallow manner. We don't read web pages, we scan them. We look for bullet points, headers, page titles, anything that will give us a quick read on whether or not what we need is on this page. Better yet, the page is so short and simple that the header and perhaps one sentence are all we need before moving on. We aren't picky. We stop when we have found something that, on the basis of our superficial decision-making, we can identify as good enough ("satisficing," in web design language).[35]

Continued use of the Internet for taking in information develops thought processes that emphasize rapid decision-making and shallow thinking.

It can be no other way. Our working memory capacity does not change; we are stuck with 2–4 items before something gets bumped. The number of choices on a web page far exceeds this capacity, so information is continually coming in and getting dumped. We are in a semi-constant state of cognitive overload. Since nothing stays in working memory very long, we never learn anything, because the consolidation process never gets started.

It is stressful. Time ping-ponging between web pages induces a state similar to what you experience when you have had too much coffee. You might not notice your hands shaking, but you will notice that your attention will not settle down on anything for more than a second or two. Deep focus and concentration—the first step in attentiveness— are impossible.

If all we want is data, a random tidbit of information for whatever purpose, then the Internet does its job well. But if our goal is real learning, then we have a serious problem. The Internet rewires our brains in a manner that is inconsistent with, and detrimental to, our ability to sustain our attentiveness at the levels necessary to effectively jump-start the consolidation process.

Consider that while the Internet rewards thought patterns that are quick and shallow, your academic work is built around *depth*. Your assignments are designed to take you deeply into a subject. There is a simple reason: depth is the only path toward mastery. Depth requires sustained attentiveness, focus, and engagement, and these are required to create new knowledge—new patterns of association between new information and existing memories—in your brain.

When your brain optimizes for the Internet, it does so at the

[35] Steve Krug. *Don't Make Me Think: A Common Sense Approach to Web Usability.* New Riders, Indianapolis, 2000
The most readable of several references on how we really interact with Web pages. His presentation makes it clear that the habits encouraged by the Web medium are in direct opposition to those required to engage deeply, i.e., to really study.

expense of your ability to engage deeply with a book, a lecture, or any other medium. The better you are at surfing the Net, the harder it will be for you to engage deeply with your Physics problem set.

This does not make the Internet bad. I like that I can book a plane ticket in mere minutes, save time and gas by ordering online, and search a forum or two to find out how to fix my motorcycle. Work is made easier through online access to databases that allow me to find the specific journal article I need in almost no time. But it is not the tool to use when I need to *learn*.

The problem does not discriminate by age. Working adults are subject to these effects to the same level as college undergraduates. *Be aware of the challenges so as to make technology the servant, not the master.*

The first step is to be conscious of your Internet use. Try keeping a log of how you use the Internet. Nothing fancy; simply write down start and stop times and what you did on the Internet for that session. Try to keep this up for a week.

I performed this experiment on myself. The results were depressing. It took only the morning to realize that I had an issue, if not a problem. I would interrupt myself constantly to check e-mail, or satisfy whatever little bit of intellectual curiosity was floating around in my head at the time. There were also instances of getting sucked into the black hole of the Web, unconsciously following link to link in pursuit of ... what? When I finally became mindful of what I was doing, I was mildly depressed. How much time had I wasted in pursuit of interesting but ultimately useless trivia?

You must make your own decisions as to how, when, and how much technology will be a part of your life. Not making a conscious decision allows the convenience and addictive aspects of the Internet to waste far too much of your time. The Internet will be in charge, not you.

As a start, make Internet and computer time a discrete task or assignment that gets scheduled. This is most likely to happen as part of research work. Stick to your schedule, and when you are done, get off the Internet and shut down the computer.[36] If you have downloaded journal articles or other references, save a copy on the computer but print a copy to read later. Avoid reading on the screen; it is too slow and too fatiguing.

Put a limit on checking e-mail, social media, etc., by checking it only once or twice a day. If you have implemented your "channel" strategy as discussed earlier, you know where to find the important stuff. The rest can be safely ignored.

My experience might be helpful. To break my Internet dependency, I scheduled everything I needed to do online as discrete tasks, on

[36] An example of high irony is that there are technological solutions for dealing with technology over-use, at least for Internet and Web-related activity. Leechblock (http://www.proginosko.com/leechblock.html) is a good example; there are many others. Experiment, but don't waste too much time looking for the ideal techie solution. Just turned the damned thing off.

index cards. I limited checking e-mail to once a day, usually in the late afternoon. I told friends and business contacts that if it was urgent, call me.

The first week was rough. Fighting the constant urge to fire up a browser window to check e-mail, social media, anything to reassure me that the world still knew I existed, was draining. But by the end of a week, it became liberating. I completed more work, it required less energy, and life was less stressful. Nobody seemed to mind that I did not respond to e-mail in five minutes. The phone rang occasionally, but after a week or two it slowed down, as people realized that I really would respond to e-mail within 24 hours, and the problem might be important but not life-or-death urgent. I quickly came to enjoy the absence of my computer or cell phone pinging with every inbound messsage.

I like the Internet, and technology has its advantages. But it is now kept securely on a short leash, a reminder that it works for *me*. Do the same for yourself, in whatever way works best for you.

Keep Planning in Perspective

People new to the idea of active time management and conscious decision-making get enthusiastic. They pursue it with vigor for a few weeks. Then life intrudes or they fall victim to temptation. They abandon the discipline for a while, fall behind, endure the stress, and then conclude the system does not, and cannot, work for them—their life is just too unique to be "managed."

We discussed the remedy to this—creating a feedback loop with a few people who can help you stick with it. But there is another trap that can snare the beginner. For some people, their calendars become an obsession. If the calendar is not perfectly up-to-date all the time, they worry and create their own stress. They spend time—too much—rearranging, rewriting, shuffling, and playing with their system. It *must* be perfect, or they fear they will not be in control. You would think that these people would be productivity ninjas, but they are not. At the end of the day, they get very little done.

This is the planning trap, and it is another form of procrastination. We have skirted this issue in earlier chapters.

Planning your work in your calendar has three objectives. The first is to make sure that you can get everything done in the time you have. The second is to make sure that you have time for important non-academic pursuits. The third is to make sure, given a conflict between these two objectives, that you make conscious choices such that the resulting plan is workable and consistent with your priorities. The significant *benefit* of this is reduced stress and a more satisfying academic life.

The plan is an aid, a guide, a map. Like a map, it is not the territory—it is not your life. Life is the actions you perform, the things you do, the relationships you build, the skills you master. The calendar is a noun; life is lived as a verb. Plan *just enough* so that you are confident that the map is fairly accurate. Once you reach this point, get to work.

Perfection in planning is an illusion. Your plan is unlikely to survive the morning before you have to change it. This is normal, and is proof enough that obsessing over planning is a waste of time. Close enough is good enough. Get to that point, then get to work.

Be Honest With Yourself

If there is a weakness in our strategy for making good decisions and avoiding procrastination, it is in the option of re-working the plan. It is easy to convince ourselves that we can slide this here, that little bit of work there, and it will all work out just fine. Every so often it really does work, so we remember those instances as justification for doing it again.

This is a trap. For this to work consistently in your favor, you have to be able to accurately estimate how much time you will need for all of your outstanding assignments. If you are wrong on just one, the whole plan will come apart, and you will lose a lot of sleep trying to get work done on time.

Honest self-assessment is even more important during your weekly review. Given that you are looking a week ahead, the work and how much time it will require become more abstract. It is now much easier to justify a shorter-than-prudent allocation of time so that you can squeeze in a social opportunity. Make these decisions in line with your priorities, but do not deceive yourself. It will surely bite you—hard, and in a tender place—later.

Some Advice, Humbly Offered

Defend aggressively against every attempt, by anyone, to command your time.

Remember that our sense of time comes from our attentiveness, and our attentiveness is our life in that moment. Make sure you are the one determining to what you give your attention. Learn how to say "no."

When I say anyone, I really mean *anyone*. There are people in your life who hold legitimate authority—parents, faculty, superiors in a work environment, people representing various offices of government who are vested with lawfully derived, limited power. Certainly you should respect such legitimate authority. But be aware of not only who is making demands of your time, but also *for what* and *why*. Decide for yourself.

You cannot say "no" to everything, yet when dealing with reasonable authority you might still have options. If some demand on your time is being presented as mandatory, ask yourself: to whose benefit? Can you get or provide information, or whatever else is required, some other way? If it is a meeting or activity that is being forced upon you, your options may be fewer but they still exist. Perhaps you can show up early, make a point of being seen, then quietly exit when the opportunity presents itself. Bring work with you, sit in the back, make the time as productive as you can.

The pressure to conform to social norms in college can be enormous. If a social event is important to you, plan accordingly. If one is being forced on you, stop, breathe, and think—is it important to *you*? Will the venue, timing, and activity add up to an enjoyable experience? If not, decline immediately, politely, and unapologetically.

Get help sooner rather than later.

If you are staring at your work and nothing happens for ten minutes, either you do not understand the assignment (what you are supposed to do), or you do not understand the material (how to do it). Stop. Waste no more time.

Get help. Use every available resource—teachers, friends, tutoring or student support services, a friendly graduate student. Schedule it as soon as possible; juggle your calendar as necessary. In the meantime, go through your ACs and find something else you can get done now.

Respect the time of those of whom you are asking help. Prepare specific questions and be able to show that you at least tried to master the material. Do not walk in saying only "I don't get it." With college faculty, you will get away with this only once. But if you went to class and show up with specific questions and enough background to demonstrate that you made a good faith effort, most faculty will do whatever it takes to help you.

College freshmen, in particular, think it is necessary to plow through their work on their own even when it is obvious that they need help. This is misplaced pride. You do not have the time to waste. Get help now.

Plan on, and expect, to have a catastrophic hardware failure at the worst possible time.

In my undergraduate career we lived in fear of a calculator failure in the middle of an exam. Spare batteries, chargers (and a strategic seating choice near an outlet), even backup calculators were standard. This was when calculators cost real money.

If by choice or nature you do a lot of work on your laptop, then you must have a backup strategy. Computer hardware will fail. The verb choice was intentional—I did not say "might," I said "will." Data on a failed machine is not always recoverable. Worse, you cannot afford the *time* required to ship your laptop to a service center, wait for them to do what they can (if anything), and ship it back. You need to be back up and running in a matter of hours, preferably minutes.

You can save work on school computers and back it up to the cloud. Services like Google Docs or DropBox work well, but you are dependent on network access to get to your data. Make it a point to copy any important work to a USB flash drive. Unless your school has policies that prohibit them, this is likely the easiest solution. Please do not forget to take them with you. Too many times I have visited high school and college computer labs and found drives left behind in USB ports.

More sophisticated solutions depend on your particular situation and how extensively you use your computer. A USB external hard drive should be considered standard equipment. They are not expensive, and you can set it up so that an image of the entire hard drive on your computer is copied to the external drive. Should your laptop fail, this makes it easy to get a new machine productive quickly. You might be able to talk a computer science major friend into writing a short macro or shell script to automate the process.

Consider having a laptop and a notebook as backup. Notebooks are inexpensive, and it would be simple enough to back up important files from the laptop to the notebook. The advantage of this strategy is that if the laptop should fail, you simply grab the netbook and get back to work.

One student I met kept multiple laptops. This might seem extreme, but his approach is creative, and not terribly expensive over the long run. He bought plain vanilla laptops. He saved money by not getting the fastest processor and settling for a mid-sized screen. After eighteen months, he would buy another, and relegate the old one to backup status. At any point he would have three laptops, and the total cost for all of them was less than the cost of a single high horsepower machine. He kept them synchronized—they were clones of each other—and when one finally failed (it did, in a most impressive way) he just grabbed another and went back to work. Most importantly, this strategy removed any stress related to a possible hardware failure.

Data backups by themselves are insufficient. If you have hardware failure, you must be able to get back to work within 15 minutes.

Get comfortable working with paper.

I see a lot of students, especially in technical majors, who try to do everything with a keyboard. There is no question that computers are powerful tools. They are very good at storing, processing, and retrieving data. Computers are truly horrible at creating ideas, finding links between new information and exisiting knowledge, creating new patterns of information, or just playing around with thoughts just to see what comes out.

Paper is almost infinitely flexible. Ideas on paper are easy to express quickly, and if you do not like them, they are just as easily trashed. Paper is easy to store, and in the amounts you will ever use in one sitting, it is portable. It is cheap, and not prone to failure.

Paper is faster. Sketches, flowcharts, quick outlines, mind maps, and thoughtful doodling are all faster on paper. You will create more, and throw away more, more quickly with paper. You will try more ideas for their own sake—just to experiment—without being committed to them.

Take advantage of printing facilities and supplies your school might have. Paper is easier to read and has fewer built-in distractions than a Web page. Information flows from paper to your brain at a pace that working memory can handle, which avoids the problem of cognitive overload so easily created when working on the computer. This facilitates the start of the consolidation process for the formation of long-term memory. Paper causes less eyestrain, and you can read faster on paper than you can on a screen. Paper allows you to more readily mark up and annotate the material; markup on a screen is either cumbersome or impossible. Search on the computer screen, but read and study on paper.

Paper has some disadvantages. It is inexpensive but you still have to buy it. It can be lost, stolen, and is vulnerable to spilled coffee. But so is your laptop.

Analog thinking tends to be faster. Instead of trying to force your work down your laptop's throat, find a whiteboard in an unused classroom. Tape butcher paper or newsprint up on a wall and tackle a nasty problem, or brainstorm ideas for a research paper. Computer software, by necessity, has to limit *how* you think. Paper encourages alternatives. Use it.

Take care of yourself.

Seems obvious, yet every semester I see students make poor choices or do dumb things that have potentially serious consequences for their health—no exercise, skipping meals, eating a lot of junk, living on caffeine (or worse), going without sleep. Keep this up for too long, and the body will deliver a very rude, possibly painful, wakeup call. Think of the following as something like a checklist:

- Build time into your schedule to take care of yourself. Your weekly review is the best opportunity to make sure that this gets on your calendar. If the idea of intense exercise is not appealing, plan a half-hour walk in the open air at a convenient time during the day; otherwise, schedule exercise time in your calendar and stick to it.

- Schedule your sleep. You simply cannot function without a certain minimum, and you are better off if you get enough sleep at the same time every day.

- Take the time to eat well. It takes little more time to eat well than poorly. Plan to meet friends for breakfast, lunch, and dinner as a way to make sure that you do eat. Make it a positive social break; a chance to recharge both body and spirit.

- Keep up with regular dental care and physical exams. If you have a health issue that requires monitoring, schedule it and stay on top of it. No excuses.

- Attend to the necessities of daily living. Schedule a few minutes at the end of the day to keep your personal spaces in order. This does not mean white-glove clean, just a place for everything, and everything in its place so you do not waste time looking for something tomorrow morning. Schedule when you will get your laundry done. This is one time when you can multitask. You can get a lot of reading done while waiting for the dryer to finish its cycle. Clean clothes and clean linen will do wonders for your state of mind and your social life.

- Know when, and how, to stop working. Have a shutdown ritual. Put it away, file it, schedule it, reschedule it until you know you have accounted for everything. Get up from the desk. Spend a few minutes doing whatever works for you to turn your brain off; to let it slow down enough to allow you to sleep. Tomorrow is another day; a chance to make better choices, a chance to learn, grow, and continue to build the life you want. Sleep well.

- Pay attention to relationships. If there is someone important in your life, give the relationship the time it deserves. Plan this time. Make your choices and schedule accordingly. Do not forget your family. Call unexpectedly. Sons especially—you will thrill your mother beyond belief if you call and tell her you just want to talk for ten minutes. Try to remember birthdays and anniversaries, even if all you can manage is a phone call or e-mail. If you have younger siblings, don't disappear from their lives just because you went off to college. Talk to them from time to time. Let them have the benefit of your experience, especially that knowledge that came at the price of mistakes. You can still be a big brother or a big sister, even if you are not home.

- Ladies, if your periods bring a level of pain that knocks you off your feet for a couple of days, plan accordingly. Do not schedule intense work sessions for those two or three days when you know you will be operating at less than full capacity. This is a judgement call and will vary between individuals; regardless, do not put yourself in the position of having to be a Zen master of productivity when you feel like your abdomen is in a vise.

- Lastly, choose your living situation carefully. I do not have objective evidence, but I will state that living with incompatible roommates is the cause of most unnecessary stress in academic life. Campus housing options vary widely between schools, so universally applicable advice does not exist. Instead, consider a few ideas:

    1. If it is evident that you and your roommates are not compatible, then *right now* take the necessary action to change your sitation. Do not stop until you get the results you want. This may require a degree of patient persistence. Summon your inner bulldog and smile while you sink your teeth into whoever it is in Student Housing, Residence Life, Student Affairs, or whatever they call it, who can affect the change you need. You might get resistance; that dealing with roommates is all part of the college experience, that you will grow as a person, etc. Whoever originally had this idea woke up one morning and had a big bowl of stupid for breakfast. You are there to master a discipline—your major—not play amateur psychologist. This is stress you do not need. *Your* time, *your* life, and your (and your parents's) money—do not settle for less than an acceptable roommate situation.

    2. Have your own space. Try at least to have your own bedroom, no matter how small. The most common reason I hear from

students as to why they choose to move off campus is so that they can have some privacy. Your mental equilibrium needs a place, however small, that you can call your own.

3. Think hard and push *all* the numbers before you move off campus. Most college housing is dull, there are intrusive rules and policies with which you must comply, and it seems expensive when examined on a dollars-per-month basis. Off-campus housing appears to be less expensive, but be careful. Make sure you *read the lease* and include all costs. If you go to school where it snows in winter and the place is heated with oil, you will have a cardiac event when you get your January fuel bill. Cable TV and broadband Internet access come standard in most dorms; off campus you will be paying for this yourself. You will do your own cooking. Your space will be larger, which means it will take longer to do the cleaning. There may be minor maintenance chores that, per the lease, will be your responsibility. So make sure you add up all the *monetary* costs, and all the *time* costs before you head off campus. Your living situation should work for you, not cause you stress.

Afterword

Before we put this to rest, I would like—and need—to thank a few people, publicly, for their contribution. Writing a book, even one as brief as this, is a team sport, and I had a very good one behind me.

Many thanks to my wife, Bianca, and my daughter and son, Kalynda and Alex. All provided feedback, challenged assumptions, and put up with endless discussion of these ideas around both the physical and virtual dinner table. I am grateful for your patience, and your love and support.

Given that I have trouble drawing a straight line with a ruler, I am indebted to Debra Wissinger for her design of the book's cover.

Two special high school teachers shared their insight into the minds and lives of college students before they get to college. Thanks to Stacy Moses of Sandia Preparatory School and Heather O'Shea of Bosque School—both in Albuquerque, New Mexico—who utterly savaged preliminary drafts, ruthlessly and without mercy. It was wonderful. Stacy and Heather, your students do not know (yet) how lucky they are.

To this point this has been a lecture; going forward I would appreciate your help to make it more like a conversation. If you have ideas or questions you're willing to put up for discussion, drop a note to gcd@49northpress.com. I'll do my best to answer, either directly or in the website's blog. Your ideas matter; they will make the second edition that much better.

You have the tools. You understand the process. There is no more to say. You either want to walk this path, or you don't.

You will confront your true self. This is hard. You will do it for the rest of your life. It is also liberating. Decide on your priorities, make your decisions, get to work, live your life. It is that simple and that hard.

You have 168 hours each week with which to craft a life. How will you use yours?

Bibliography

David Allen. *Getting Things Done: The Art of Stress-Free Productivity*. Penguin Group, New York, 2001.

William J. Bennett, editor. *Our Sacred Honor: Words of Advice from the Founders in Stories, Letters, Poems, and Speeches*. Simon and Schuster, New York, 1997.

Nicholas Carr. *The Shallows: What the Internet Is Doing to Our Brains*. W. W. Norton & Company, New York, 2010.

Francesco Cirillo. The pomodoro technique, 2006. URL http://www.pomodorotechniqe.com.

Jon Kabat-Zinn. *Wherever You Go, There You Are: Mindfulness Meditation in Everyday Life*. Hyperion, New York, 1994.

Steve Krug. *Don't Make Me Think: A Common Sense Approach to Web Usability*. New Riders, Indianapolis, 2000.

M. Muraven, D.M. Tice, and R.F. Baumeister. Self-control as limited resource: Regulatory depletion patterns. *Journal of Personality and Social Psychology*, 74:774–789, 1998.

Cal Newport, Ph.D. The study hacks blog, 2011. URL http://www.calnewport.com.

Steven Pressfield. *The War of Art*. Grand Central Publishing, New York, 2002.

Aaron Smith. Americans and text messaging, 2011. URL http://pewinternet.org/Reports/2011/Cell-Phone-Texting-2011.aspx.

John Sweller. *Instructional Design in Technical Areas*. PCS Data Processing, Inc., New York, 1999.

Made in the USA
Lexington, KY
04 April 2015